Cavalier's Adventure
The Story of
Henry Norwood

Cavalier's Adventures

The Story of Henry Norwood

Sharon Himes

HERITAGE BOOKS
2015

HERITAGE BOOKS
AN IMPRINT OF HERITAGE BOOKS, INC.

Books, CDs, and more—Worldwide

For our listing of thousands of titles see our website
at
www.HeritageBooks.com

Published 2015 by
HERITAGE BOOKS, INC.
Publishing Division
5810 Ruatan Street
Berwyn Heights, Md. 20740

Copyright © 2002 Sharon Himes

Maps and Illustrations Copyright © 2000 Sharon Himes

All rights reserved. No part of this book may be reproduced or transmitted in any form or by any means, electronic or mechanical, including photocopying, recording or by any information storage and retrieval system without written permission from the author, except for the inclusion of brief quotations in a review.

International Standard Book Numbers
Paperbound: 978-0-7884-2072-6
Clothbound: 978-0-7884-6241-2

In memory of two mothers;
Margaret and Mary

Contents

List of Maps and Illustrations	xi
Preface	xiii
About the Maps	xv
Acknowledgements	xvii

One
  Troubled Times   19

Two
  Azores' Sojourn   37

Three
  Perilous Voyage   53

Four
  Wilderness Landing   75

Five
  Native Hospitality   101

Six
  Southern Expedition   125

Seven
  Farther Journeys   145

Epilogue   157

Bibliography   169

Index   171

Maps

Chesapeake Region	iv
England 1643	xii
Cotswold Hills	18
Downs of England	34
Eastern Atlantic	36
Azores	42
Faial	45
Atlantic Coast	52
Winds and Currents	66
Castaways' Landing	74
Kickotank Territory	100
Eastern Shore	124
Eastern Bay	134
James River	138
Western Europe	144
Norwood's Route	156
Locations Today	158
Kickotank Today	162

Illustrations

Cavaliers	23
Prince Charles	26
Royal Exchange	32
Merchant Ship	39
Fortifications	46
Toast to the King	48
Hatteras Shoals	56
Storm at Sea	61
Castaway	79
Island Campfires	84
Island Meeting	94
Native Transport	98
Queen's Welcome	104
Native Village	108
Native Foods	113
Indian Map	117
Parting Friends	129
Forest Trail	132
Hungars Glebe	137
Green Spring	140
Coronation Parade	151
Tangier	152

Preface

Several years ago I read an obscure journal by Henry Norwood, a seventeenth century traveler to the Eastern Shore of Maryland and Virginia. The old-fashioned spelling and antiquated words could not disguise a fascinating adventure and I wanted to know more. I began exploring antique maps and modern references to trace Norwood's journeys. On the way I learned about the complex world he lived in, the people he met and the further travels of this remarkable man.

I am an amateur historian, following my own curiosity with the freedom and enthusiasm of an amateur. Since childhood I have been fascinated by maps, often making my own for pleasure. I find that maps help me to visualize and explain a place in its time. Creating maps of Norwood's journey was my first impulse on reading his narrative.

Henry Norwood published his account many years after his voyage in 1649-50. He may have kept some notes along the way and filled in the blank areas from memory later. The account, published in his lifetime as a broadsheet entitled A Voyage to Virginia, has gained him acceptance as one of the important Southern writers of the seventeenth century. Cavalier's Adventure is largely based on his account. I have tried to include many of Norwood's remarks in their original context, but for reasons of clarity, I have modernized spelling and punctuation.

Norwood set out on his journey in September of 1649 and his narrative continues through the following spring. In 1582 the Gregorian calendar corrected the growing discrepancy between the Julian calendar year and the solar year. Many countries were slow to adopt the change and until 1752 England was using the old style calendar.
    The dates that Henry Norwood mentions in his account would be ten days later by today's reckoning. He also notes dates from January to March as being in the year 1649. In that period, the new year began on Lady's Day, March 25th near Easter and the first day of spring. Seasons are important to the story. To avoid confusion, I have used the modern style when mentioning dates, beginning the year 1650 in January instead of March and making the ten day calendar correction.

Henry Norwood lived in a turbulent time. The seventeenth century was a period of national war and local conflict, religious persecution and political upheaval. Western civilization was in the throes of transition between medieval and modern times. The Protestant Reformation was barely a century past.
    It is not the purpose of this book to recount the English Civil Wars. The complex tangle of royal purpose and Puritan zeal, emerging middle class and regional determination is beyond the scope of this work. Norwood was a witness to much of the history of his time, however, and his view gives us a better understanding of

the changes taking place. He was educated and well read. Born a year before Shakespeare's death, he was alive at the same time as John Milton, Galileo, Rubens and Francis Bacon. Samuel Pepys, who knew him, mentioned Henry Norwood several times in his famous diaries.

About the Maps

Travelers have used maps for many centuries and the art of cartography has evolved. In the early 1600s maps were accurate only in a general sense. Most ships had charts to plot their course, but navigation was primitive and map making was more an art than a science.

Map makers, who were usually not sailors themselves, used earlier maps as the basis for newer ones. While information from returning ships often gave corrections and improvements, the errors in one map usually were passed to the next.

It was 1665 before ocean currents were depicted on maps. Sailors steered by compass or star positions and determined latitude by the height of the sun. Longitude was still a mystery. A ship headed toward America would sail due west until land was sighted and then go north or south to find its destination. Because of this longitude problem many early maps seem to be stretched north and south and out of proportion.

Politics often affected map making. Spanish map makers did not put England on their charts when the two countries were at war. Disputed areas were exaggerated or mislabeled, and there was no uniformity of names for many places. Nautical hazards were usually well documented, but areas of little importance commercially or nautically were often ignored or inaccurate.

From the time of the discovery and early settlements in the New World, maps show changes and growth. What is left out often tells us as much as what is included. Often the same maps were reprinted many times, with new corrections and additions every time returning ships shared what they had learned. The progress of settlement can be seen in the additional names and improved details that were included in each successive edition.

Henry Norwood had only a vague idea of his location when he landed in the wilderness somewhere between the civilized areas of Virginia to the south and the settlements of the Dutch to the north. His ideas were based on the maps he had seen and none offered any details of that region. We have only his observations and other research to guide us in estimating his location. Like most of history, Norwood's story is just that, a story, based on research, conjecture and hopefully more than a touch of truth.

The maps here are drawn to scale and based on modern sources, including satellite imagery. That does not imply ultimate accuracy, however. The impact of climate, tides, human activity, and other factors combine to make it unlikely to get a truly accurate view of what any area was like in 1650.

These maps are only meant to guide the modern traveler on a voyage of imagination. They are designed from Norwood's perspective, and include primarily what was known in his time, but use names and spellings that are more familiar today. The spelling of Indian names, however, varies with the source. In most cases I have chosen to use Norwood's version of Indian place names. His phonetic spelling was what he heard firsthand from those who lived there.

Acknowledgements

It is not an easy task to discover information about the life of an individual who lived 350 years ago when he was not a major historical figure. I am grateful for assistance and suggestions from a variety of individuals and organizations as I searched for Henry Norwood.

It is thanks to Kathy Fisher, Director of Furnace Town Historic Site near Snow Hill, that I was introduced to Norwood's story. Her extensive knowledge of the area has been invaluable. I am grateful to Reggie Bunis, who assisted with research in Philadelphia and Williamsburg.

I must acknowledge the help offered by several libraries and research centers. The Research Center for Delmarva History and Culture at Salisbury State University in Salisbury, Maryland provided access to their collection on the history of the Eastern Shore, including the Bessie Holloway Collection. The Rockefeller Library at Williamsburg, Virginia included much of the information on Jamestown and life in Virginia in the mid-seventeenth century. I first read Norwood's account at The Worcester County Library in Snow Hill, Maryland, where I centered my research.

Jerome and Alex Ryan, Marilyn Bookmyer, Dorian Smith and many others offered helpful insights and materials on sailing and other aspects of the story. Internet friends in Portugal, England and the Azores gave me a wider view. Mary Humphreys edited the final version. Marilyn Freeman helped with early editing and Jeanne Frank assisted with publishing.

My deepest gratitude is to my husband Larry who supplied ideas, encouragement and a belief in my quest. Although distant in more than time or relationship, Henry Norwood has been almost a part of our family.

18 *Cavalier's Adventure*

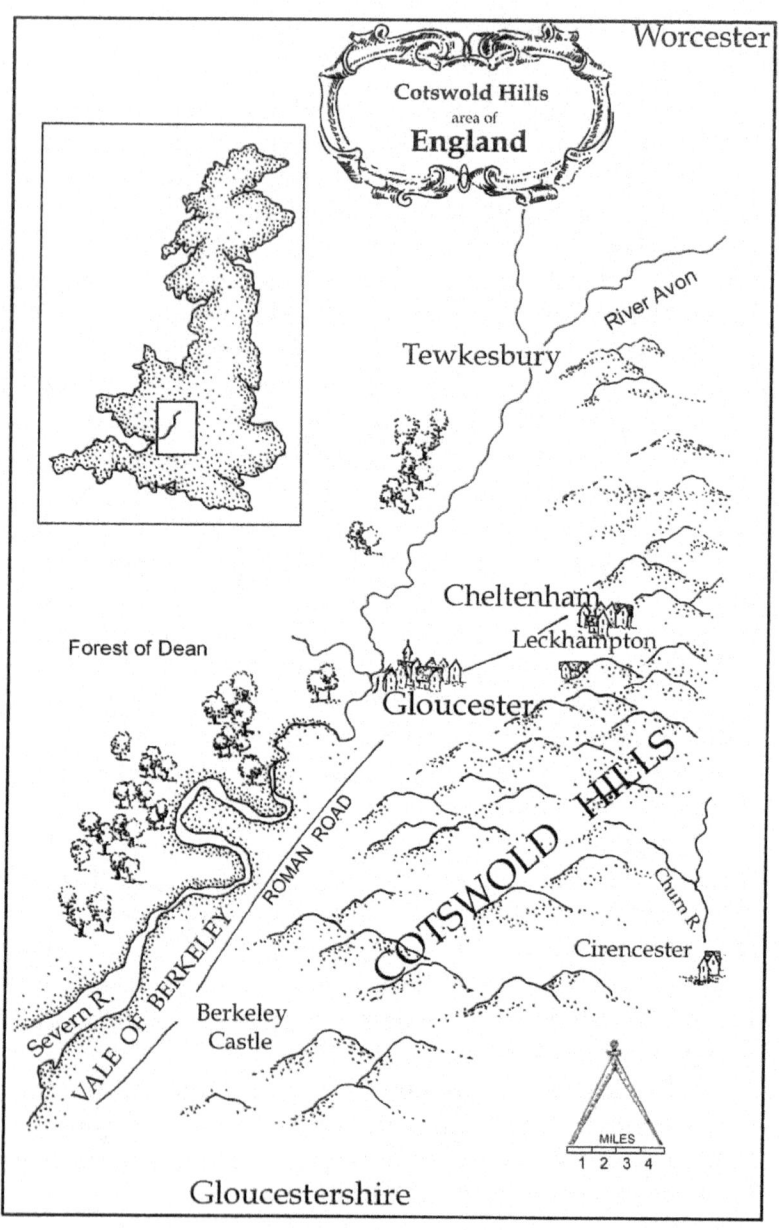

One

Troubled Times

"TO OVERCOME IS TO LIVE"
The personal motto of explorer, colonist and historian, Captain John Smith, might serve any who dared set out on a voyage in the seventeenth century.

With a last glimpse of England disappearing into the sea behind him, a man had only his own courage, intelligence and luck with which to face unknown dangers ahead. The rocking ship beneath offered only timber and tar between life and a watery grave. Sickness, plague, starvation or violence were only a few of the perils that abounded on land or sea.

A voyage across the Atlantic to the young colony of Virginia might take five weeks or much longer. Passengers had to endure bad food and uncomfortable surroundings and threats of sickness or storms. A man who had said goodbye to friends, family and home to face unknown dangers abroad, must have had good cause.

Thirty-five-year-old Henry Norwood was such a man. He had read the writings of Captain John Smith, and the explorer's motto "to overcome is to live" is one Norwood might have borrowed for his own.

There were not many prospects for a young man in the seventeenth century. Henry Norwood was born into an English family with aristocratic connections, but he was the younger son of a younger son. English laws were written in such a way that only the eldest male heir could inherit land. The younger sons, landless and with no future in farming, had to find other occupations.

Social position was inflexible. Every man had his place and was likely to be punished socially if he left it. A family's history, connections, religion and occupation established the status of its members. Thus, Henry Norwood's position in society was set when he was born to parents with important family connections, but little property.

Henry Norwood's grandfather, William, was the influential owner of Leckhampton Court, a manor house near Gloucester in the west midlands of Britain. The Norwoods were also related to the important Berkeley family in the castle near the Severn River. This heritage of family position and noble connections was impressed on the young Henry, who was expected to follow his father's footsteps into law or government service.

Henry Norwood's father, Henry Norwood, Esq., was a barrister who had been educated at Oxford. In 1598, during the reign of Queen Elizabeth I, the elder Henry went into law practice with James Kirton of Somerset. They had a moderately successful law practice in a small town.

Eleven years later his partner died. Shortly afterward, Norwood took the practical step to marry his partner's widow, Elizabeth. Elizabeth was the daughter of Sir John Rodney of Somerset, one of the wealthy founders of the Virginia Company which had established Jamestown in the young colony of Virginia in 1607.

The couple had two boys, first Thomas and then the younger Henry, who was born in 1615. Before Henry was a year old, his father died. The family was then living in the county of Somerset, south of the Norwood family home. There are no records to indicate if the widow's financial status would have allowed her to remain independent. In the seventeenth century, it is more likely that after her husband's death, Elizabeth and the children went to live at the Norwood family home at Leckhampton Court, two miles south of Cheltenham. It was that corner of Britain where Henry felt most at home.

Gloucestershire is an area of lush river valleys and steep ancient hills, often topped with standing stones, picturesque castles, or Roman forts. The landscape has been populated for over four thousand years and was densely settled even in Roman times.

The Leckhampton Court manor house nestled at the base of Leckhampton Hill on the edge of the Cotswold Hills, an ancient region of western England. Leckhampton Hill itself was a landmark, with an Iron Age hill fort and limestone quarries. The honey-colored stone of the Cotswold Hills was the common building material in grand homes, small cottages, churches, and miles of fence walls. The grasslands offered good grazing for nimble footed sheep. The Cotswold area, dotted with sheep farms, was known since medieval times as a wool-producing region.

The Norwood family was nearly as established as the rocky hills. They were closely related to the noble Berkeleys, residents of Berkeley Castle since 1153 and one of England's oldest families. The castle, a Norman fortress by the Severn Estuary, was the meeting place for barons on their way to persuade King John to sign the Magna Carta as well as the scene of the murder of Edward II in

1327. By the seventeenth century the heritage of both families included ties to the royal cause.

Life was not peaceful or prosperous in the early part of the 1600s. Crop failures and a rising population were adding to unemployment in the area and the countryside was uneasy because of the growing conflict between King Charles I and Parliament.

Charles was the son of James I and like his father a strong believer in the Divine Right of Kings. The king felt that his position was a sacred duty and none on earth had authority to challenge his rule. This feudal tradition of royalty as providers of order and continuity was in variance with those who wanted self-determination and more local government. A growing merchant class saw more profit and stability in rule by an elected parliamentary body and various religious sects resented interference from any source. As the population began to take sides, conflict was inevitable.

Often the distinctions between *Cavaliers*, royalist supporters of the king, and *Roundheads* as the parliamentary supporters were called, were obvious at a glance. Cavaliers were men of fashion and style. They often dressed in a tunic of silk or satin with slashed sleeves and an elegant lacy collar. A short cloak was worn over one shoulder and short, full trousers reached to the top of wide, high boots. A broadbrimmed beaver hat was often decorated with a fancy band and a plume of feathers.

Cavaliers wore their curled hair to the shoulders and a neat beard was trimmed to a point. At court it was fashionable for a Cavalier to wear a long lock of hair on the left side, called a lovelock, tied with a ribbon. The Cavaliers were often well educated and enjoyed poetry and literature along with formal, elegant manners. They enjoyed gambling, dancing, horse racing and theater-

Cavaliers

going among other entertainments. They were usually supporters of the Established Church.

The Puritan Roundheads were so named because they wore their hair close-cropped and straight. They usually dressed plainly in somber tones, usually wearing a plain linen collar, a cloak of brown or black and a high crowned hat. Puritans tolerated no recreation except singing of hymns or reading of Psalms and regarded almost all amusement as frivolous or sinful. According to their philosophy, life was serious and only hard work would result in prosperity, a sure sign of God's favor.

The contrast between serious Puritans and frivolous Cavaliers was far from black and white. Religion was an integral part of society but the choice of which church or sect was more the result of an accident of birth or education than conviction. Most agreed there must be none but an official religious opinion, the question that caused problems was what Church should be *the* Church.

The two sides were not strictly based on class divisions or religion and there were representatives of all levels of society on each side, sometimes dividing families and friends. In general, London and the south and east of the country were rich with a large merchant class which supported the parliamentary side. Royalist supporters tended to be in Wales and the north and west of England. The Norwood family held a strong belief in the monarchy and remained loyal to the king throughout the growing conflict.

A childhood was short in the 1600s. Half the population was poor and had little education. In the early part of the seventeenth century only 30% of men and 10% of women could even sign their names. Most boys were apprenticed by the age of fourteen. Sons of the upper class were better educated and were taught Latin and Greek along with more traditional subjects. Books were still relatively rare and expensive so memorized speeches and oral tradition provided an important form of education and entertainment.

Since the younger sons would not inherit family estates, they were often destined for civil or military service. For the young and energetic Henry, the future lay in the military. It is probable that his grandfather helped him gain a commission in an influential royal regiment.

It was expensive to purchase a commission and equip a man with the dramatic costume; sword, and armor that a Cavalier was expected to wear, but such service added to the family honor.

Henry was seventeen when his grandfather, William Norwood, died in September of 1632. By that time, he had completed his education and had a commission in the king's service. Norwood went with his regiment to fight in Ireland and he took part in many battles early in the Civil War. By the time he was twenty-five in

1640, he had risen to the rank of major and was likely serving under his neighbor and kin, Sir John Berkeley, fighting for the royalist cause.

King Charles I, firm in his belief in Divine authority, was in perpetual conflict with a House of Commons that wanted to limit his rule. In 1629 he had dissolved the Parliament and revived old taxes and collected tariffs without their approval to support the government. Although he succeeded financially, his policies were bitterly resented. Royal courts persecuted Puritans and thousands fled from England to establish colonies in North America.

In 1637 Charles tried to force the Scottish Presbyterian subjects to accept Anglican church ritual among other reforms. The Scots resisted and the king had to summon Parliament to raise funds to support an army. Parliament met but refused to give money unless the king agreed to a series of measures to limit royal power.

In 1642 tensions had grown worse when King Charles attempted to arrest five members of Parliament. They escaped before he arrived, but soon both the king and Parliament were stockpiling weapons and gathering troops for an English Civil War.

By 1645 young Charles, Prince of Wales, at the age of fourteen, was in nominal command of the Royalist operations in the western part of England. Older advisors surrounded the young prince, but he was an important figurehead to rally the troops to the royal cause. His father may have thought his heir was safer in the west where there were more Royalist supporters.

One of the three commanders with the forces under the prince was Sir John Berkeley, who was headquartered at Bristol. Henry Norwood, a young educated and cultured Cavalier serving under Berkeley, probably met the young prince on various occasions. In May of

Charles, Prince of Wales

that year a plague struck Bristol, and the command with the prince at its head, was hastily shifted to Barnstable, farther to the west.

Under the able leadership of Oliver Cromwell, Parliament's army was the first professional military. The forces were composed of merchants, tradesmen and small farmers. They were well paid and equipped from tax money voted by Parliament. This newly organized and disciplined cavalry force became known as the *Ironsides* and soon the entire Parliamentary force was reorganized into the *New Model Army*.

Without tax money to support them, the king's diminished regiments were forced to live off the land and were only financed from what money they were able to get from the sale of the queen's jewels and donations from supporters. On June 14, 1645 Cromwell's army soundly defeated the royal forces at the important Battle of Naseby.

Many towns and villages in the West Country suffered devastation as battles raged through and around them. Parliament held most of England and eventually turned its full focus to defeating the remaining loyalists in the west. In spite of many victories, Cromwell was unable to capture Prince Charles who escaped to the Scilly Isles in March of 1646.

The tiny islands off the southwestern edge of the country were but a temporary refuge. When Parliament's ships surrounded the island, only luck, in the shape of a brisk wind, saved the day. The ships were scattered and the seventeen-year-old prince was able to sail with about 300 followers on to the Jersey Islands near the coast of France. After a few months they went on to the palace of St Germain-en-Laye near Paris where the prince's mother, Queen Henrietta Maria, was a guest of her parents, the King and Queen of France.

The French agreed unofficially to host the prince. It was to their advantage to gain the favor of the English, or at least keep them from becoming an enemy while they were involved in an expensive war with Spain. For two years, St Germain was the rendezvous point for Royalist exiles, and Charles was the center of a variety of plans to help his father recover royal control of England.

In May of 1648, John Berkeley was made the governor for the younger Prince James, and the party settled at Rotterdam in The Netherlands. Norwood was probably still with the group, since it was in the fall of that year that Henry Norwood met with two friends, Richard Fox and Francis Morrison, in a tavern there. Rotterdam was a haven for exiled Englishmen and many had established businesses in The Netherlands.

The friends met to consider their future plans. Prospects seemed bleak for Cavalier interests. King Charles, who had turned to the Scots for help to retake his kingdom, had instead been delivered to Parliamentary forces. He was being kept under guard at the Isle of

Wight. The young Cavaliers, to whom the king was a sacred leader, were appalled at the treatment accorded their monarch. They agreed to persevere in the king's service until the following summer, at least. Without pay or support they would not be able to stay with the army indefinitely. By August they would meet again to assess the situation and decide what plans to make regarding their own futures.

A few months later, in January of 1649, King Charles I was brought to trial in London. In a tribunal controlled by Cromwell's army, the king was summarily found guilty and executed. The news reached Europe in early February that the king had been beheaded, and the young Prince of Wales was declared to be King Charles II by his shocked and bereaved Royalist subjects. Gaining his father's throne in England would be a daunting task.

Prince Charles was eighteen when his father was beheaded. Surrounded by advisers and supporters, he was determined to retake the throne. Almost immediately the Scottish Parliament declared him Charles II, lawful successor to his father. Before it was agreed to crown him in Scotland, however, Scotland's leaders wanted to impose conditions. While the prince made plans, he chose to stay in Holland. Charles's elder sister, Mary, was married to William, a prince of The Netherlands, so the young man felt secure in that country. A king in name only, Charles was without finances, an army or a throne.

In March of 1649 Scottish commissioners arrived at The Hague with demands and concessions for the new king. Many of the conditions were politically unacceptable to Charles and his supporters. By the end of May, negotiations with the Scots had gone from bad to worse. Charles notified the Dutch States General that he would reject Scottish offers.

The royal court was expensive to maintain in exile, since the king had to be kept in the luxury that was appropriate to his status. Although his mother had sold her jewelry, and some money came from supporters, they had no income from England. Hundreds of courtiers attended the prince to care for his wardrobe, apartments and stables. Even without pay, the servants had to be provided with food and housing. The remaining military men had not received pay in many months. Advisers and other Royalists paid their own expenses.

Charles asked the Dutch government for money so the court could depart for Ireland. The Dutch, who recognized Charles as king of the Scots, but not ruler of the English, were unwilling to give him any money. The English court in exile was at a standstill.

At about this time, Colonel Henry Norwood decided to take his leave of the remnants of the Cavalier army and word of his planned departure came to the ears of the young king. In a period when a young uncrowned King Charles II felt his kingdom slipping through his fingers, Henry Norwood was likely to have been seen as a useful agent to ask for help from Royalists in the Colony of Virginia. The Commonwealth government of England under Cromwell had not yet had time to gain control over far-flung colonies and Virginia still supported the exiled king.

Norwood met with Charles and was given a letter of introduction to the Governor of Virginia, William Berkeley. Berkeley was a staunch Royalist and a relative of Norwood's, as well as younger brother to Norwood's former commander, Sir John Berkeley. Unlike the Puritan-ruled colony of Massachusetts, Virginia had never submitted to the new Commonwealth of Oliver Cromwell. Charles knew that many former Cavaliers were now planters in Virginia and remained faithful to his cause. Their financial support was vital to reviving a Royalist military and providing weapons.

In the later account of his voyage, Norwood mentions only a letter of introduction from the king. Since he was a known and trusted officer, it is likely that he was also given other letters and instructions to take to the government in Virginia. By his later actions, it is apparent that Norwood took these letters and instructions very seriously. He knew that his beleaguered monarch was depending on him.

In June of 1649 Norwood returned home to England to settle his affairs. In Gloucestershire he was met with hostility from representatives of the new government. The Puritan Parliamentary Committee ruled for Cromwell's regime and maintained control over the remaining Royalist sympathizers. Repressive laws and punitive taxation made it difficult for Cavaliers to return to their homes or remain there. Oaths of allegiance were required and extra taxes and fines were imposed on any who had fought on the side of the Royalists.

On his arrival home, Norwood was summoned to Goldsmith's Hall where the Parliamentary Committee charged him with having fought on the side of the king during the Civil Wars. In spite of his objections, Norwood was fined fifteen pounds. In England, under the Commonwealth, it was a serious crime to be a supporter of the exiled Charles II, or even to speak of him as the king. By fining Norwood, the Parliamentary Committee reinforced his intent to leave the country for good.

In August of 1649, as they had arranged the year before, Henry Norwood met his friends, Francis Morrison and Richard Fox, in a London tavern. The three were unanimous in their intent to leave England and to set out for Virginia. Their determination had strengthened since their last meeting in The Netherlands.

If prospects had seemed bleak a year ago, when news was reported that King Charles I had been imprisoned on the Isle of Wight, the news of the sovereign's beheading in January was more than the young Cavaliers could bear. All of Europe had been shocked by the news of the execution of an anointed king.

Royalist friends and sympathizers were so appalled by the action that many preferred to leave England at all costs. As Norwood phrased it, they preferred to "fly from their native country as from a place infected with the plague." Any point on the compass might better suit their interests than to remain in England, the Cavaliers declared.

Many of those of nobility, gentry and clergy who were able, set sail for far-flung colonies and foreign lands. Those who had money or credit chose to try their fortunes in Surinam, Barbados, Antigua, and the Leeward Islands. A fortune could be made on large sugar plantations in those places, but the expense of milling machinery and slave labor was high.

Those without financial backing often chose to make their way in the wilds of Virginia. Jamestown, begun in 1607, was the first permanent English settlement in America. After forty years dealing with hostility from natives, poor crops and an unhealthful site close to the river, the town was was struggling, but outlying farms were beginning to prosper. The Chesapeake Bay area was growing quickly with large and small farms producing tobacco and other crops for export.   The area of the James River was populated with friends and relations who had done well.

That Norwood and his companions had little

Royal Exchange

money was not the only reason they chose Virginia as their destination. Norwood explained to his friends that he was related to the governor of the colony and had a letter of introduction from the king. "My best caragaroon was his majesty's gracious letter in my favor, which took effect beyond any expectation, because it recommended me to the governor's particular care." The three friends agreed to depart together for Virginia as soon as possible.

Near the tenth of September 1649, they met at the Royal Exchange in London. The Exchange, a forerunner to today's stock market, was a busy bazaar; open on three sides, and crowded with stalls, peddlers, business and finance of all kinds. There they met with Captain John Locker. A posted announcement told them Locker was captain of the ship, *Virginia Merchant*, soon to sail for America.

After a short discussion, the party agreed to pay six pounds a head for themselves and their servants for passage to the James River in Virginia. Their goods would be transported in the hold at the going market rate, the captain explained. The price was quite reasonable, considering that the going rate for transportation in that period was seven pounds. Passengers were considered a form of cargo, and for a voyage to Virginia late in the shipping season, any cargo was welcome.

The *Virginia Merchant* was a three-masted ship of 300 tons burden weight, designed wide and high to carry stores of tobacco leaf from Virginia to merchants in England. The ship would need to be loaded with as many goods and passengers as possible on the westward leg of the trip, if only for ballast. Without enough weight in the hold of the ship, it would ride too high in the water like a cork. Insufficient weight would make the ship hard to maneuver and unstable in heavy winds.

Around the twenty-fifth of September, Norwood and his friends met on the dock at Gravesend to deliver their goods for loading. The port of Gravesend was about twenty-five miles down the Thames River from London and offered deepwater portage for larger merchant ships.

The *Virginia Merchant*, like many other vessels in the tobacco trade, timed the voyage for maximum profits for their owners and investors. An autumn crossing increased the chances of running into bad weather in the North Atlantic. There was always the possibility of a late hurricane or early winter gale, and most ships preferred to be settled in a secure harbor for winter.

In the Chesapeake Tidewater region, tobacco was harvested and cured in the autumn. The first leaves were available in October with the bulk of the production ready between November and January. Ideally the Atlantic crossing could be made in seven or eight weeks. The captain of the *Virginia Merchant* hoped to time his arrival with the readiness of the crop in mid-November when he could then spend the winter in Virginia. The arrangement, if perfectly timed, meant cured tobacco would

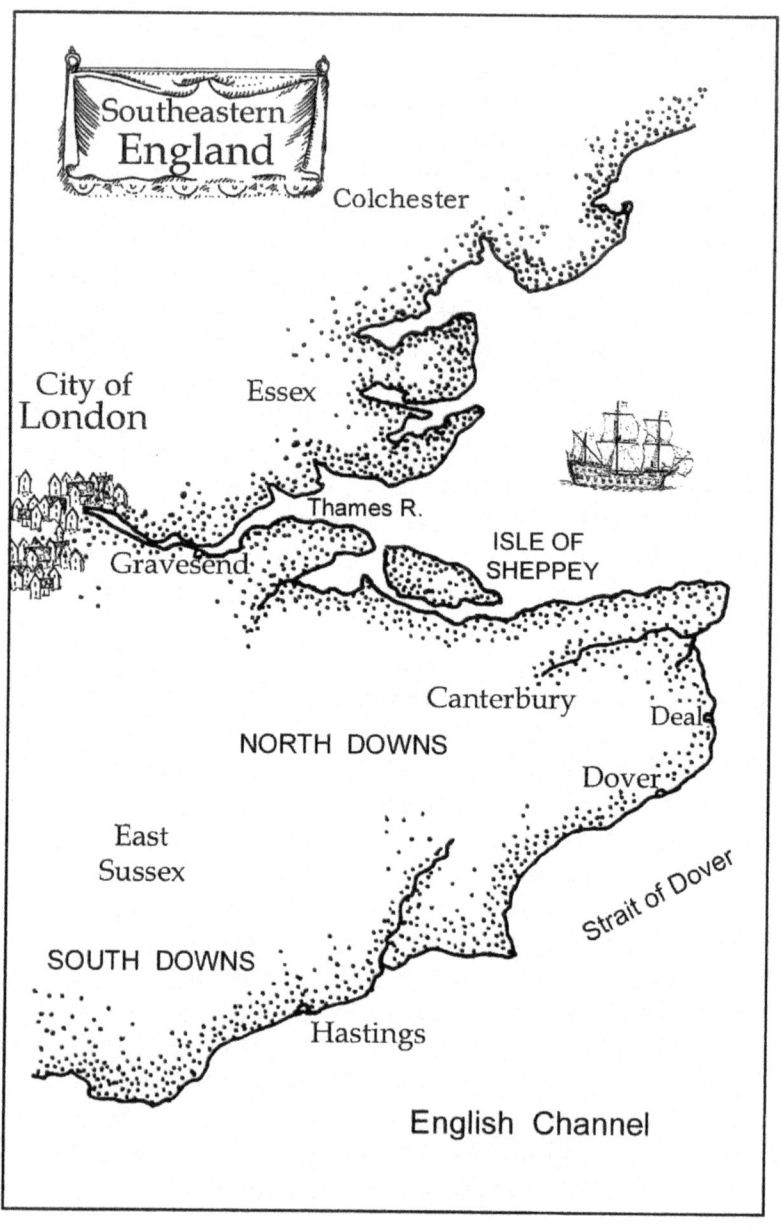

arrive in the markets of England when prices for fresh leaf were the highest. Ship owners depended on the skill and timing of a vessel's captain, who would share in the profits from a successful trip.

Rather than spend the last days on the ship while it was being prepared for departure, Norwood's group took a post coach for a region known as the Downs on the southeast point of England. There, where the Thames River meets the English Channel, they watched as the *Virginia Merchant* joined dozens of ships assembling in a protective convoy.

The lawless seas were dangerous in the seventeenth century, and ships tried to sail together to help each other in case of attack. On the *Virginia Merchant*, thirty guns; heavy iron cannons, provided protection against enemy ships. It was standard practice to carry enough ammunition for at least two battles on an Atlantic voyage.

As the end of September neared, the assembled ships were forced to stay anchored offshore while waiting for winds to shift. The English Channel is notoriously difficult for sailing ships to navigate as they had to contend with frequent heavy fogs, dangerous tides and fickle winds.

Norwood and his party lodged at an inn in the town of Deal for nearly a week while they waited, impatient to be gone. They had almost used up their ready expense money by the time the wind at last veered to the east, and they were summoned by flags and guns to come aboard. The three Cavaliers were rowed to the ship, and took leave of their native land with little expectation of ever returning.

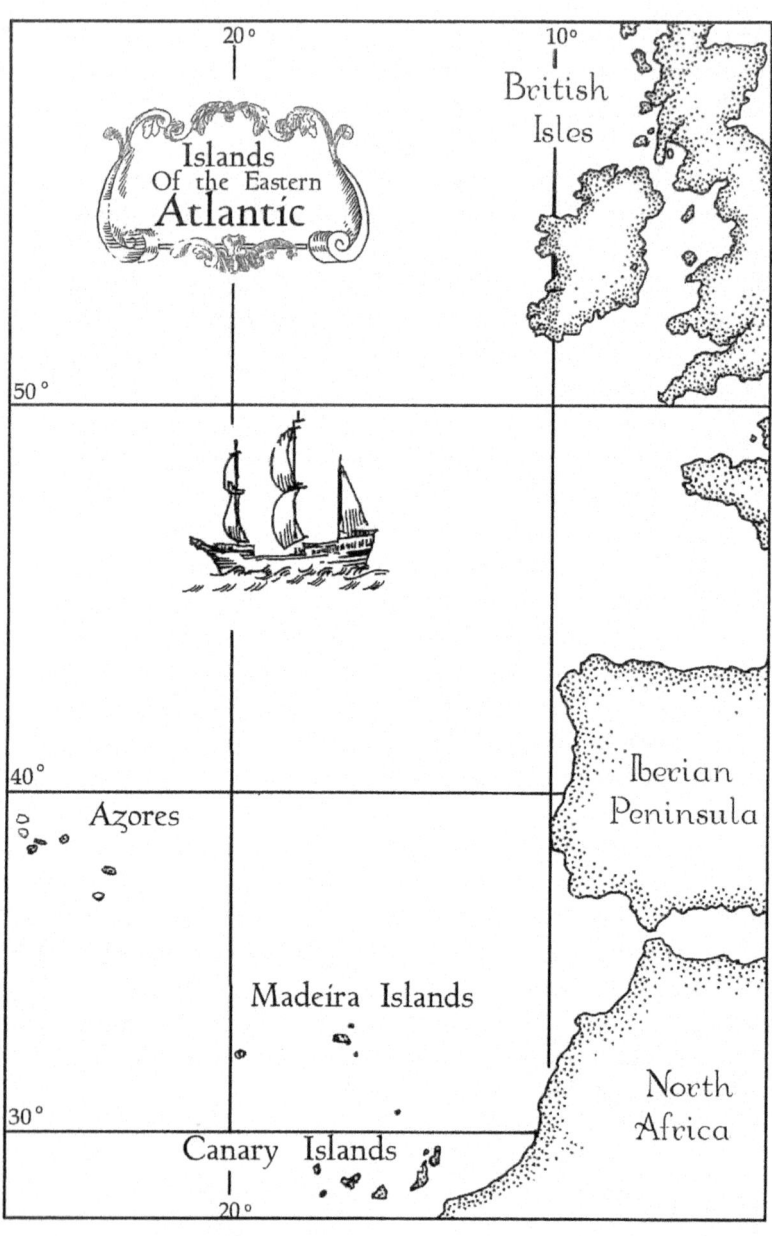

Two

Azores' Sojourn

On board, space was at a premium as it was on any ship. The *Virginia Merchant* was a moderate sized commercial vessel carrying three hundred thirty people; officers, passengers and crew. Little provision was made for their comfort, but privacy was an unknown luxury on land or sea in the seventeenth century.

Norwood's group was given accommodations on the quarterdeck in the aft of the *Virginia Merchant*. There they were allotted space in the area used by the officers for sleeping, navigation, mess hall and meeting room. This special treatment, though not luxurious, may have been due to their social standing or, more likely, an extra payment to the captain.

Their cabin consisted of a canvas partition surrounding a six by six-foot wooden platform. A rough mattress filled with straw provided the bed that all three shared. They were entitled to eat with the captain and officers, and likely brought their own provisions of meat and wine to supplement the menu.

While Norwood and his friends resided in relative luxury above them, their servants were quartered below them on the lower deck. There they had a canvas partitioned space with other passengers and livestock and where they could keep watch on their masters' goods.

Most of those heading for Virginia in the mid-seventeenth century were young people eager to make a living on the tobacco farms in the New World or fleeing harsh Parliamentarian rule at home.

The tides of emigration began in 1607, increased in 1620 and after 1629 became the flood referred to historically as the Great Migration. At the time of Norwood's voyage, many of the passengers would have been recruited from Gloucestershire near Norwood's family home.

Craftsmen and laborers were always in short supply in Virginia and the accents of the West Country would have been heard throughout the ship. Many who faced unemployment or starvation at home were enticed by promises of a rich new world described by agents eager to fill ships with a profitable living cargo.

Those who could not afford passage money were contracted as indentured servants. If they survived the voyage their contracts would be sold in Virginia. After working four or more years to fulfill their contract, the immigrants would be then be free to build their own futures in the new land.

The rough sailors who operated the ship were likely English but many may have been from other European countries including Holland which was known for shipbuilding and sailing. The men worked long hours outdoors in all weather, slept in shifts on cramped bunks, and often ate bad food.

They probably still saw it as a better life than what was available on shore in a time of war, plague and famine. Sailing a ship was a craft, a livelihood and adventure.

Seventeenth Century Merchant Ship

Over two hundred passengers made the voyage below decks. They were required to bring their own bedding and other supplies for the voyage. Canvas tarpaulins partitioned spaces for families, livestock and belongings. The canvas could be drawn back during the day, opening the area for conversation and allowing for movement. Lanterns hung from the low beamed ceiling to provide a little light in the dim room, but they could not be used in rough weather. A few ports let in air for people and animals, but were often closed against the sea.

Privacy was nearly unknown in the small dwellings that sheltered their large families on land. Cramped and uncomfortable lodging on a ship packed with animals, humans and other cargo may not have been much worse, except for the incessant rocking and pitching on the waves. The design of a merchant ship caused it to move constantly in even a peaceful sea. Seasickness was nearly universal and unwary passengers often fell or were flung against hard surfaces by the movements of the ship.

Fire was dangerous on the wooden vessel, so no cooking could be attempted below decks. Two cooks slept in the galley with the pots in the forecastle, or nose of the ship. There they kept watch on a hearth fire set in a bed of bricks and sand. Food for sailors and passengers was simple fare and usually served at noon, a time considered to be the beginning of a new day.

Passengers were encouraged to bring up to five pounds of provisions per person to supplement the meager diet. Peas or beans were boiled in a large kettle with a little salt pork as a regular ration and individuals might add pepper and other flavorings they had brought with them.

Simple biscuits made with lard and rough flour were a staple food on ships. Since baking was not an easy task at sea, the biscuits were usually cooked on shore and stored in casks for the journey. Often the biscuits were months old and sometimes eaten by shipboard rats, or infested with insects. The cooper controlled the ship stores and rationed fresh water, which was carried in barrels deep in the ship's hold to serve as ballast as well as provision.

When the *Virginia Merchant* finally set forth into the English Channel in convoy with other outgoing ships. Henry Norwood recorded, "We had a fresh large gale three days, which cleared us of the channel and put us out of soundings."

Apparently untroubled by seasickness, he watched the activities of the ship's crew with interest. Each day a lead weight tied to a heavy rope was dropped overboard by sailors. The rope was marked in fathoms of about six feet, and a sounding of the water depth was reported to the officer of the watch. On the third day the plummet line no longer touched the sea floor, and they knew they were out of the English Channel and in the Atlantic Ocean.

Navigating an Atlantic voyage to America in the seventeenth century was primarily a matter of keeping a ship pointed toward the west. Using a compass and observations of sun and stars, the navigator was able to determine accurately the direction of travel. There was no wheel to control the rudder. A kind of heavy stick, called a *whip staff* provided rudimentary steerage. The direction of travel was primarily controlled by the set of the sails.

A knotted line with a float was dropped into the sea to help estimate speed. As the ship moved forward, leaving the float behind, the regularly spaced knots were counted as they passed through a sailor's hands. Using the number of knots that passed in a specific period of time, the speed of the ship could be estimated. A knot is approximately 1.15 statute miles (1.85 kilometers) per hour. There was no way to determine wind speed or the effects of ocean currents on a ship.

It would be nearly a hundred years before there would be any way to determine longitude. That measurement depended on having a clock that could withstand sea conditions and remain absolutely accurate.

Timekeeping on a ship in 1650 was still kept by an hourglass which was turned when the sand ran out. The navigator carefully recorded the time, direction, and estimates of speed in the ship's log book.

Even with the disadvantages of navigation in that period, a good sailor could direct a ship to within thirty miles of his destination. Hundreds of merchant ships of all sizes went to and from the Americas on a regular basis. Many plied the same routes for years. Shipping was a profitable business.

After the Virginia Merchant had been sailing for about three weeks the ship's cooper, who was in charge of

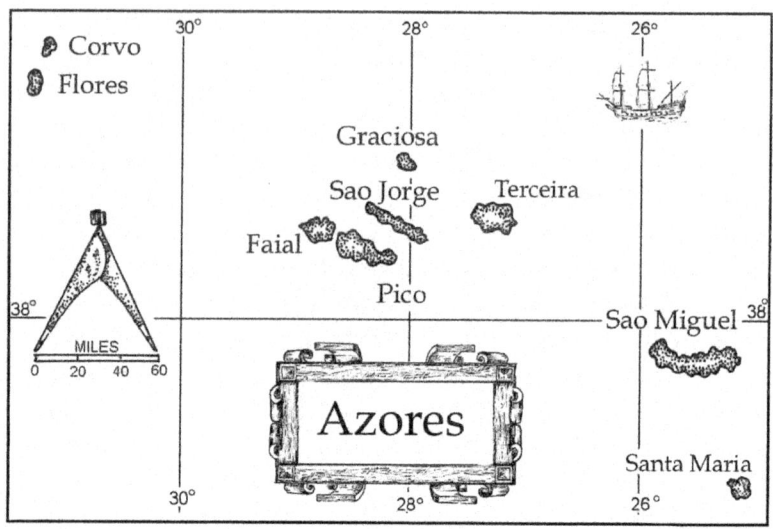

ship's stores, went to the captain. One of the cooper's most important jobs was to ensure that there was enough drinking water for the passengers and crew. He explained to the captain that the week's delay in starting out had seriously depleted their water supply. Even with favorable winds, the voyage would still take at least another month, he pointed out. There would not be enough water to last the large company all the way to Virginia

Since Norwood and his friends were quartered in the room where the officers met, they were privy to all the discussions that took place there. The Cavalier listened as the master, who was head navigator of the ship, expressed his concern over the water situation.

Calling in the other officers, they looked over the charts. It was determined that the ship was likely near the Azores or Western Islands. The Captain ordered the ship to turn south immediately, and sailors climbed the rigging to look for sight of land. Faial, with its volcanic peak, would probably be the first land they would see, the navigator told Norwood.

Since that island had a good port, it was decided to land there to resupply the ship with water and other provisions. When informed of this stopover, the passengers were delighted to gain even a brief view of land. After weeks of boredom below decks in a dim and cramped space, any change of routine was welcome.

At daybreak of October twenty-fourth, the lookouts gave a shout and pointed to where a peak showed on the horizon. A seaman explained to Norwood that Faial was the highest and most conspicuous landmark in the Atlantic besides Tenerife, largest of the Canary Islands. Faial's volcanic cone of Cabeco Gordo rises in a dramatic point to an altitude of 3422 feet.

There are nine volcanic islands in the Azores Archipelago in the mid-Atlantic, about 932 miles from Europe and 2423 miles from North America. The islands were discovered in 1427 by Portuguese sailors who found no native population. A few years later settlers came from the mainland, and by 1500 there were people living on every island.

The ship sailed directly for the harbor of Horta on the southeastern coast of the island of Faial. The port is landlocked by the peak of Monte da Guia about a mile east of the town. As they stood on the deck approaching the island, Norwood and his friends saw a landscape of steep rocky cliffs, green valleys and low hills. Dramatic black sand beaches ringed the island.

The moist autumn air was comfortable as they sailed into view of the castle fort. The ship fired her guns in a salute to the castle and an answering salute came from another English ship anchored in the harbor.

Soon after the *Virginia Merchant* dropped her anchor English merchants from the town came on board. One of them, Mr. Andrews, proposed a dinner party where they could taste of the fruit and meat of the island.

Norwood and his two companions were invited to Mr. Andrews' house, along with the captain of the *Virginia Merchant*. Also invited was Captain Tatam, master of the ship that had saluted them, the *John*. Norwood was introduced to Captain John Tatam, who told him he was recently returned from Brazil in the service of Portugal. They were bound for Lisbon, he told them. The *John* carried a rich freight and a noble lady who was returning to Portugal with her family.

As they were served an elegant dinner at Mr. Andrews' home, their host explained to the visitors that the climate is mild in the Azores, and some fruits and vegetables could be grown all year. However, the weather can be highly variable, he told them. Morning sun often gives way to heavy showers at noon. By afternoon the humidity can be stifling, and strong winds bring a sharp drop in temperature at night. Autumn and winter rainstorms are frequent, and the natives foretell the weather by observing the clouds around the volcanic peak of Pico Island to the east.

After dinner Mr. Andrews invited the guests to visit his peach trees for dessert. It was a rare treat for young Henry Norwood, who was particularly fond of peaches. He admitted that he took at least a double share of the ripe fruit. As they were staying overnight with Mr. Andrews, Norwood was able to return in the dead of night to the peach orchard to "satisfy a ravenous appetite nature has too prodigally given me for that species."

The next morning the visitors were given a tour of the island. Although settled by Portuguese, the Azores

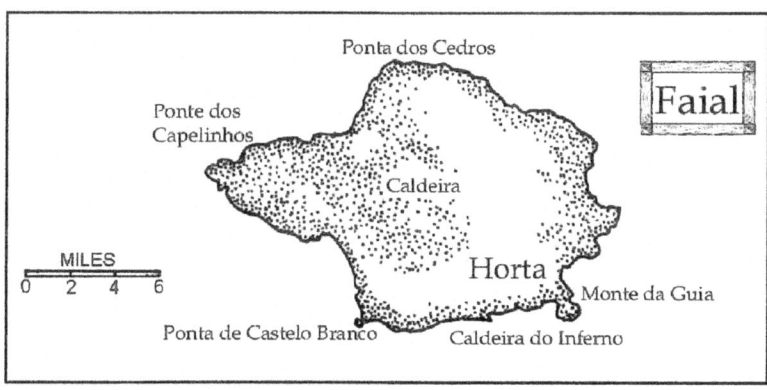

were occupied by Spain early in the sixteenth century during a war between the two countries, the visitors were told. The unprotected islands became prey for pirates in the Atlantic. A Spanish fleet captured Faial in 1583. Since Spain was at war with the British and French, pirating ships from those nations had attacked the island. Invaders ravaged the defenseless island, burning and pillaging and leaving a trail of violence.

By the 1640s the returning Portuguese began building fortifications around the island. Norwood and the other visitors toured the new castle fortress overlooking Faial's major town and port, Horta. With the experienced eye of a professional soldier, he determined that the port was well fortified with guns in good position to guard the seacoast. Plans called for a ring of forts, linked by a road around the nearly circular island.

The group was invited to meet with the Portuguese Governor. In a formal audience, the Governor told his English visitors that he had recently received a command from the King of Portugal to treat all ships that remained faithful to the exiled king of Great Britain with more than common courtesy. Monarchies of Europe, while slow to offer any financial help to an exiled Charles, nevertheless sympathized with the England's royal family, to whom many were related.

After a day spent touring the sights of the island, Captain Tatam invited the party to a dinner aboard his vessel. When time neared for the dinner, the Captain sent his boats to the guest house to bring the visitors to his ship. It was a good thing he extended them this courtesy, Norwood remarked, for "our ship's longboat having been staved in pieces the night before, by the seamen's neglect, who had all tasted so liberally of new wine, by the commodiousness of the vintage, that they lay up and down dead drunk in all quarters, in a sad pickle." Apparently the drunken sailors had neglected to secure the longboat, and it was bashed against the hull of the ship and lost. The longboat was the only sizeable vessel in case of emergency and the one remaining small wherry could not carry a fraction of the passengers. There was nothing that could be done about repairing or replacing the lost boat until they reached Virginia.

The loss of the longboat made the process of delivering barrels of fresh water to the ship more difficult

Fortifications

and costly. Every day of delay increased the probability of being caught in an early winter storm. The captain was eager to sail away as soon as possible.

He ordered island boats to be hired to bring water and other provisions to the ship. The captain left the job of supervising the work of reloading to his officers and ordered them to use all diligence, and greater care than before. Meanwhile he went with Norwood and others to visit the other English ship.

At their arrival on the *John* they were met formally with the salute of a whole volley of cannon from the ship. Captain Tatam, dressed in his finest attire, welcomed them on board and served his visitors excellent wines. "There was a handsome plenty of fish and fowl, several ways cooked, to relish the Portuguese and English palates; and, which made our entertainment more complete, he had prevailed with that great lady, with her pretty son of about twelve years old to sit at the table with us."

A dinner party in the seventeenth century was often a long and formal affair with many courses and a variety of foods brought ceremoniously to the table one at a time. The flavors of Portuguese cuisine would probably have been too spicy for English tastes. Meats, marinated with wine and olive oil spiced with cayenne and paprika may have been unusual or even unpleasant to those accustomed to a bland English diet.

Strong spices used by Portuguese cooks helped preserve foods in a warm climate and upper classes could afford more of the imported spices. Even the wines of the region were fortified to prevent spoilage. The meal would have included several meat and fish courses, with vegetables and fruits more as garnish. Potatoes and tomatoes were yet unknown but roasted chestnuts, figs and olives are still traditional in Portuguese cuisine.

Toast to the King

For Norwood, the highlight of the meal was the female guest, the Portuguese lady of an important family, who ate with them. She was dressed in a heavy silk gown with an ornate lace collar that defined her high social position.

"She was taller than the ordinary stature of that nation, finely shaped, had a very clear skin; her eyes and hair vying for the blackness and beauty of the jet; her modesty served, without any other art, to put a tincture of red upon her face; for when she saw herself envisioned with a company of strange faces, that had or might have had beards upon them, her blushes raised in her face a delicate complexion of red and white."

As a passenger of noble birth, she was accorded the distinction of eating with the officers, but it was unusual for an unaccompanied woman to eat with strangers. On a crowded ship, however, there was not enough room for her to dine alone, so she was the only female at the Captain's dinner party.

Her son, about twelve years old, accompanied her. The Englishmen were politely surprised that a boy of that age would be permitted to sit at a formal dinner with adults. It was nearly unheard of in poor or noble homes in that period. Children were considered unformed adults in miniature and were usually seen only by relatives or servants.

The captain acted as interpreter. Through him, the Cavaliers expressed to the lady how honored they felt to make her acquaintance. Norwood commented politely that they realized that she was forced to admit them into her presence, since there was no other place on the ship fit for her to retreat while the strangers were visiting the ship.

The lady's son attracted the attention of the Royalists. They whispered among themselves that the shape of the youth's face made him look like the young King Charles when he was that age. Finally the group broke out with the comment and made a great deal of their admiration of the resemblance. As King Charles' grandmother was from the Italian Medici family, both shared Mediterranean coloring.

They drank the health of the kings of Portugal and England to the accompaniment of peals of cannon. The boy was permitted to drink a small portion of the toast to the English king that he was told he resembled. The lady felt this comment on the appearance of her son to be an honor, so she ordered more wine to be brought, and they repeated the health of the kings in a rich wine from Brazil.

The party was a great success, but approaching night forced the party to close sooner than the guests would have preferred. Merchants had warned them that it was unsafe to walk the streets of Horta at night, and said they should return to their lodgings in the town before dark. They were told of *Pycaroes*, a kind of land pirate, who would often accosted strangers in the city to snatch hats and looser garments and disappear into the shadows.

The Englishmen thanked their host and asked him to translate their compliments to the Portuguese lady and her son. She returned their courtesy with her wishes for their happy voyage.

While the party continued all afternoon and evening on the *John*, the *Virginia Merchant* made little progress in restocking its supplies.

"Whilst we were caressed in this manner on shipboard, the seamen on shore continued in their debauchery, with very little advance of our dispatch; the getting water was so tedious in itself for lack of our boat, and so full of delays by drunken contests of ours with the islanders, and with themselves, that, after some days' stay upon the island, when our captain resolved to sail away, he found the ship in worse condition for liquors, than when we came on shore, for if we had a new supply of water, the proportion was hardly enough to balance the expense of beer that was spent in the time we got it."

As there was no way to keep water pure or safely drinkable over a long voyage, beer was considered a form of pickled water. While there were new barrels of water stowed in the ship's hold, the beer was so much depleted that the actual supply of liquids on board was not much better than when they had turned the ship to detour to Faial. From the Azores to Virginia would be expected to take at least five or six week yet and the passengers and crew of the ship would have no further source of water unless they were able to collect a little rainwater.

Another detour to the only other islands near their route, the Summer Islands (Bermudas) would be impractical. The time for dangerous winter storms was approaching and it was important to cross the Atlantic without further delay.

Some days before they left the Azores, Norwood and his friends watched the *John* under sail bound for Lisbon. Norwood later learned that after Captain Tatam arrived in Portugal and discharged his ship, he had enlisted his ship as a man of war in a squadron under Prince Rupert fighting for the Royalists. The prince, whom Norwood knew in later years, told him Captain Tatam did his duty well.

About the first of November the ship was finally ready to continue toward Virginia. Norwood expected to eat well for the remainder of the voyage. "We had store of black pigs for fresh meat, and I carried peaches without number."

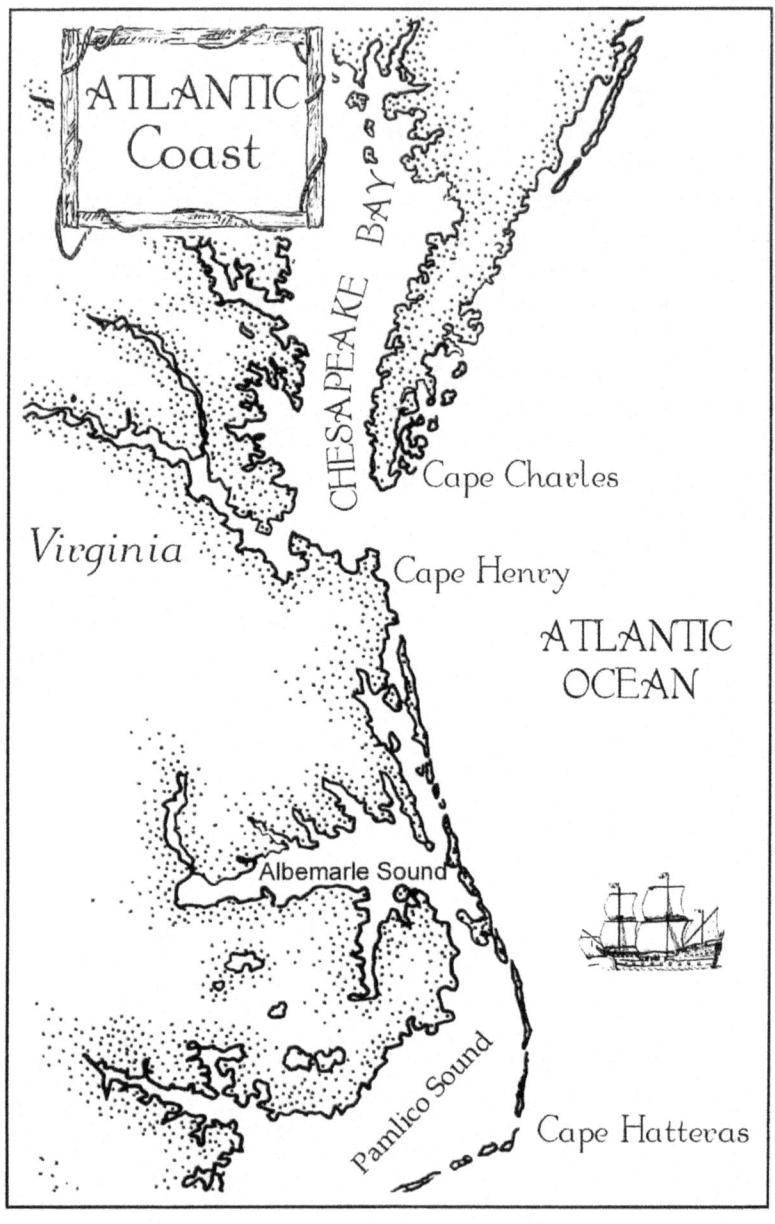

Three

Perilous Voyage

The ship left the Azores and caught a favorable breeze that soon took the ship into the trade wind. The trade winds are strong prevailing winds of lower latitudes and were considered dependable for moving a sailing ship westward toward the Americas. The winds that the *Virginia Merchant* caught shortly after leaving Faial were brisk enough to push the ship at the rate of fifty or sixty leagues (90-120 miles) in twenty-four hours. Soon they were at the latitude of the Bermudas according to the Captain's map.

The ship tossed on a turbulent sea. The sailors explained it was their general observation that at that latitude the seas are usually rough and the weather stormy. They were unaware that the cause was the warm Gulf Stream that pierces the cold Atlantic waters at that latitude. The seas are generally rough in that area.

Even in port the ship rocked severely. In the rough seas of the eastern Atlantic with a strong wind billowing the canvas sails, the ship vibrated with stresses of wind and sea and thick ropes hummed with the tension. While Morrison and Fox most often stayed below, ill with seasickness, the younger Norwood, apparently untroubled by the motion of the vessel, enjoyed walking on the deck and observing the activities of the sailors.

One afternoon an officer of the watch pointed out a spot on the stormy sea. It was an agitation of the water in one place that slowly built up force until a great waterspout sprang up violently. Watching the phenomenon, Henry wondered "that there was force enough to have hoisted our ship out of her proper element, into the air (had the helm been for it) and to have made her do the supersalt (somersault)."

Soon they had a glimpse of the Bermudas. It was a sight especially welcome to mariners because they then knew exactly how far it was to Hatteras in America from that point. The passengers were pleased because they knew it would not be long until they would be safely delivered to the James River.

The gale continued until November eighteenth, and then they saw the water take on the distinctive dark blue that marked the warm water of the Gulf Stream. Dropping the lead-weighted line, sailors determined that they were sailing in thirty-five fathoms of water. It was another happy indication that the ship was nearing its destination in the New World.

Before dawn the next day Norwood woke early. "Weary of my lodging, I visited Mate Putts on the watch, and would have treated him with brandy but he refused that offer, unless I could also give him tobacco which I had not. He said, it was near break of day, and he would look out to see what change there was in the water. No sooner were his feet upon the deck, but with stamps and noise he calls up the seamen, crying out, "All hands aloft! Breaches, breaches on both sides! All hands aloft!"

The sailors, hearing this alarm, ran on deck in a

moment. In the growing light of early morning they could see the extreme danger all around them. Frothing water showed where low sandbanks caught the waves and caused the water to break, or 'breach' over them. . The ship was in imminent danger of running aground and being torn apart on the Hatteras shoals as so many other ships had done.

In a moment the deck was in turmoil. "The seamen were soon on deck with this dismal alarm, and saw the cause therof; but instead of applying their hands for their preservation (through a general despondency) they fell on their knees, commending their souls as at the last gasp. The captain came out at the noise to rectify what was amiss but seeing how the case stood, his courage failed."

Mate Putts, pulled himself together and took heart again and cried out, "Is there no good fellow that will stand to the helm, and loose a sail?" There were only two men in the entire crew who would obey his call for help. Thomas Reasin and John Smith (no relation to the explorer) ignored the cries of the others and set to work at Putts' commands. The undisciplined and uneducated sailors had heard of ships that had broken up in this infamous region and had probably never heard of a ship that had escaped such a fate.

John Smith climbed up and loosened the foretopsail so it would catch more wind to make the ship easier to steer. On a sailing vessel where steering is accomplished about eighty percent by the set of the sails and only twenty percent by the rudder, it must have forward movement to have any steerage from the rudder. Tom Reasin stood to the helm and at the last moment was able to turn the large ship from the starboard breach. The cumbersome ship, made to carry heavy cargo, was far from maneuverable, but for once answered the helm.

Hatteras Shoals

No sooner than they were safely away from one bank than they were headed right for another. By this time most of the other sailors began to believe they might yet escape this predicament. Soon all were rushing about to help handle the sails, and they were able to again steer away from certain disaster. As the full light of morning finally broke forth, they saw the ship surrounded by breaches with scarcely any channel water to avoid them. Suddenly a tremor ran through the ship as it struck ground and raised a crash of water and sand together which fell on the main chains.

All worked frantically to keep the ship afloat. Tom Reasin, seeing the most likely water for a channel, ordered the helm. Again and again, they threw the leaded rope over the side and rejoiced when it showed the water a little deeper as they went. Farther into that new channel, against all odds, there was eighteen and then twenty feet of water; more than enough water to float the ship.

As the morning advanced to full day, the quartermasters were able to con the ship and soon they were miraculously clear of the deadly breaches at Cape

Hatteras. Once the ship was out of danger and clear out to sea, the seamen looked around "like so many spirits they surveyed each other, as if they doubted the reality of the thing, and shook hands like strangers, or men risen from the other world, and did scarce believe they were what they seemed to be, men of flesh and blood."

Soon they were working to set the sails for seaward, and a brisk northwest wind came to assist in moving the ship away from infamous Hatteras shoals. The gale soon grew to a violent storm, however, which increased in intensity. Winds began separating the ship from the land at the rate of eight leagues a watch although only the small forecourse sails were set to help steering.

The master of the ship thought it was necessary to stop that course as soon as possible. They were heading southeast, away from their intended port. He ordered the officers to bring the ship about and to furl all the sails and to try with the mizzen to return to a heading toward Virginia. The forward sails on a three-masted ship provide the propulsion while the triangular mizzen sail on the third mast at the back of the ship is used for steering. In an excessive wind, most sails are taken down to keep them from being damaged.

The seamen struggled to work the ship about, but the seas towered over the ship, and the waves were too rough to accomplish it. They were already a long way from land and something had to be done to stop the ship from continuing to run away at such an excessive rate of speed. The square sails hung from yards, or horizontal beams. In a strong or contrary wind the sails are furled or rolled up along the yard and in a very heavy wind some of the yards themselves can be taken down. The *Virginia Merchant*'s sailors lowered the main yard to ease pressure on that mast and laid it on the ship's deck. The greatest difficulty was how to deal with the foresails so the ship might be able to turn safely or at least with as little risk as possible.

All the men together were not strong enough to pull the foresail closed. Many immense mountains of water crashed on the ship as it worked through the trough of the sea, struggling to turn. Norwood was with his friends when one wave "chanced to break upon the poop (where we were quartered) and that with so sad a weight, that I've guessed a ton of water at the least did enter the tarpaulin, and set us all on float who were in the roundhouse. The noise it made by discharging itself in that manner, was like the report of a great gun, and did put us all into a horrible fright which we could not soon strike off."

Out on the heaving deck, the mate still worked to turn the ship. He knew that when all sails come down but the mizzen, the ship would automatically turn head to wind because the wind pressure would push the mizzen downwind. In spite of the rough sea, sailors, clinging to wet ropes managed to tie up the foresail so it could not catch the wind. At last the ship came about with the mizzen pulling her stern to leeward. With wind and seas still high, the *Virginia Merchant* was at least striving to head toward land with only the mizzen to guide her through a growing storm.

As evening approached to end the terrifying day, Norwood stood on the deck with the tired seamen. "I cannot forget the prodigious number of porpoises that did that evening appear about the ship to the astonishment of the oldest seamen in her. They seemed to cover the surface of the sea as far as our eyes could discern; insomuch that a musket bullet, shot at random, could hardly fail to do execution on some of them. These the seamen would look upon as of bad portent, predicting ill weather, but in our case, who were in present possession of a storm, they appeared too late to gain the credit of foretelling what should come upon us in that kind."

In growing darkness the sea around them was enraged and all in foam. The gale increased as the storm intensified, and the ship bobbed on the rough ocean like a tall cork. Since Norwood and his friends were quartered in the roundhouse where the captain made his office, they were privy to the frequent reports made by the officers on watch. As the voyagers listened, they were very concerned to hear that the storm would wreak some serious damage to the ship before it was over.

Near ten or eleven at night as the *Virginia Merchant* struggled through pitching seas, a crash echoed throughout the ship. All hands were called with loud cries to the deck. The fore-topmast had crashed to the deck. It had not fallen by itself, but also brought down the foremast head which was broken off short, just under the cap.

It was a dangerous situation as the ropes and rigging of most of the ship depended on the stays and tackles fixed to that mast. A sailing ship is carefully balanced with the tensions from ropes and pulleys. Without some of this network, the ship is unstable and harder to control. Mate Putts expressed his belief that more disaster would soon follow. The loss of rigging and mast would be nothing to what was yet likely to befall them said the mate. In all likelihood the storm would end with the sinking of the ship.

The ship was still buffeted by gale force winds and violently tossed from wave crest to trough as midnight passed. Putts was on deck shortly after when he heard the sea break with a boom on the foreship near where he was walking. He scrambled back to safety up to his knees in water. As he made his way to the relative safety of the roundhouse, he was muttering short prayers, sure that the ship was foundering at her last gasp.

Every seaman was convinced this terrible storm brought death. The *Virginia Merchant* had been pitching violently for hours. Suddenly, with a shudder, the ship stood stock still with her head under water, seeming to bore her way into the sea. Norwood and his companions, huddled together on their sleeping platform, shared the terror of every passenger and seaman on board. "My two comrades and myself lay on our platform, sharing liberally in the general consternation. We took a short leave of each other, men women,and children. All assaulted with the fresh terror of death, made a most dolorous outcry throughout the ship."

Meanwhile, Mate Putts, still on duty, saw that the deck, tilted sharply, was almost cleared of water. He called for sailors to man the pumps. All the water that washed over the decks and into passageways and other openings accumulated in the bowels of the ship and had to be pumped out quickly to keep her afloat. The general opinion was that pumping was a waste of time and the deepest part of the ship an unpleasant place to die.

Unlike his two companions, Norwood had good sea legs and was glad of an occasion to go out and find out what damage had been done. He made his way to the deck in spite of the howling dark night and rolling of the ship. It was a terrible sight. The entire forecastle at the front of the ship was gone, broken off by the sea. Six of the heavy cannons were gone and all of the anchors except the one fastened to a cable. Since the galley was in the forecastle, the cooking supplies, food, and two cooks were also washed overboard. Norwood was amazed to learn one of the cooks was recovered by a strange providence,

Storm at Sea

but he doesn't elaborate on that miracle. Perhaps the lucky man was washed back onto the ship after being cast overboard.

The loss of the forecastle made a great gap in the nose of the ship. If they could not find a way to cover it, the opening would let in even more of the violent sea. Luckily, the *Virginia Merchant* was carrying a number of passengers who were land carpenters on their way to work in Virginia. Several volunteered their skill and in spite of the violent motion of the ship, in a little time they had built a rude platform to hold back the water.

The tempest continued to grow more intensive in the early hours, and more efforts were needed to prevent even more serious damage. The bowsprit had lost all the rigging and stays that kept it steady. It swayed to and fro with bangs and crashes on the bows. It would have to be cut close to prevent more damage to the ship. The deck of the ship was in miserable disorder. The danger increased since stays of all the masts were now gone. The shrouds that remained were loose and useless. It was easy to see the main topmast would soon crash down upon them.

Tom Reasin, who was always ready to meet the dangers, ran up with an ax in his hand and attempted to ease the mainmast. The danger was too great, and he was called down. No sooner was his foot on the deck than both main and topmast all came down together. In one crash, all fell to windward clear into the sea, and not one person was hurt.

The mainmast had fallen broadside into the sea but it was likely to be even more dangerous in that position. The shrouds and rigging were still attached the mast to the ship even as it lay perpendicular to the hull. Every wave caught the mast as it dragged beside them, and it became a battering ram against the wooden ship. Each vibrating thud was answered by an echoing cry from the passengers below decks. Sailors ran for axes to cut the ropes. The storm had turned even the suffering ship against herself. Norwood watched as the frantic sailors worked to chop away the ropes and at last freed the ship from the dangerous mast at her side.

For the darkest hours, the ship was totally at the mercy of a furious sea. Masts broken, rigging cut, the *Virginia Merchant* was no better than a half-destroyed hulk and barely afloat. With no rigging to keep the ship steady, the seas tossed it up and down. "Our seamen frequently fell overboard, without any one regarding the loss of another, every man expecting the same fate, though in a different manner." In many tumbles, the deck would touch the sea and stand still momentarily as if it would never rise to ride another wave. The passengers below decks, tied to their platforms, were in the most terror of their lives. The water-soaked wooden planking creaked and screamed as if alive. Fear, darkness and violent movement, crashing and moaning combined to make a living nightmare.

By morning light the storm slackened and the crew began to assess the damage. Only the mizzenmast remained at the back of the ship. It was still hoped the ship could be brought about when the winds were more cooperative, but winds were still blowing strongly from the west and still pushing them farther away from their destination. The twenty-third and twenty-fourth of November passed with no improvement. On the morning of the twenty-fifth they saw an English merchant ship. She showed her flag but would not approach, even though the storm had abated.

Norwood listened with interest as the officers, after a discussion, decided that the merchant ship had been afraid to be civil. Although the *Virginia Merchant* looked severely damaged, she still had more guns than the other could resist. The other may have been afraid the *Virginia Merchant* would attack them to take whatever they would not sell or give. The stranger shot a gun to leeward, stood her course, and turned away to make a smaller target in case of attack. The *Virginia Merchant*, which was in no condition to pursue them, watched the other ship limp into the distance.

Before making the attempt to turn the ship back toward the Americas, it was necessary to refresh the seamen. They were almost worn out with work and lack of sleep. No one had been able to eat set meals for many days. The passengers, after days of terror and discomfort in the storm, had no appetite.

The state of the remaining food stocks was deplorable. The storm had destroyed the galley in the forecastle along with the cooking hearth and utensils. Water had flowed in to the storage area and much of the bread flour was ruined by seawater. There was no way to dress the meat. Without her rigging to steady her, the ship continued to pitch and tumble making any efforts to set a cooking fire most dangerous.

It was decided to try to make a fire below decks. The carpenters sawed a large cask in two and filled one half with ballast where they hoped to safely set a small cook fire. This was done, and a pot of beans was set to cook. Several times, in spite of great care, the improvised hearth was overturned by the pitching of the ship, and the cooking process had to be begun again.

About the twenty-seventh of November the seas finally began to abate. Several other ships saw the *Virginia Merchant* and were seen by her, but would not come near. Only one would approach. She was also severely damaged by the storm and kept the pumps going constantly. The ship lay by, and the *Virginia Merchant* sent a party by way of the wherry, their only remaining small boat.

The master of the other ship showed the visitors his ship's leaks which were serious. He could not offer the *Virginia Merchant* any aid, but asked for men to help him keep his own pumps going. Both ships were nearly helpless and promised to keep each other company since they were headed for the same port. In the darkness of another cloudy night, however, the ships became separated, and the other was never heard from again.

By November twenty-eighth the weather had calmed sufficiently to allow the crew to attempt to turn the ship around. Using the mizzenmast to turn the ship was complicated by her lack of forward sails to balance the turn. The stern would turn more readily than the damaged forward part of the ship. It took considerable skill and no less luck to get the clumsy hulk to respond to commands, but eventually they succeeded.

Having finally turned the *Virginia Merchant* back toward the Chesapeake Bay, the next problem was how to make sail. The foremast still stood steady, although damaged. It was necessary to fix a yard beam to it in order to attach a sail. Nearly three feet thick, the wet and greasy stump of a mast would be difficult for any to climb. There were no ropes left attached, and no one could help from below. A fall from the heights would likely cost a man's life.

Some of the passengers watched unhappily as crewmen discussed the problem, discouraged by the predicament that faced them and at a loss as to how to proceed. Then the sailor, Tom Reasin, came forward and volunteered. The passengers were eager to encourage him in the dangerous attempt. They promised to reward his service handsomely. Once they were in Virginia, they said, they would richly reward him in tobacco. The amounts of their promises were all the more generous because they never expected to make land. Henry Norwood commented "The proportions being set down, many were the more generous, because they never thought to see the place of payment, but expected to anticipate that by the payment of a greater debt to nature, which was like to be exacted every hour by an arrest of the merciless sea, which made small show of taking bail for our appearance in Virginia."

Tom Reasin found half a dozen iron spikes among the scattered parcels of the ship's stores. First he drove one of them into the mast at about the height of his head. When that was done he took a rope about ten feet long and having threaded it in a block or pulley to divide it in the middle, he made both ends meet in a knot on the spike. The rope was thus draped on both sides of the mast, so that the block falling on the opposite side became

a stirrup to climb on for driving another spike the same way.

Tom Reasin climbed with many of the anxious ship's company watching from below. Step to step, cautiously waiting for the smoothest part of the sea to strike his hammer, the sailor gained the topmost part of the mast. He drove cleats to fasten the shrouds, lines that would be a hold for others to climb. Soon more seamen were high above the ship. They raised the broadyard and then fastened a sail to it. In only a few hour's time, the ship was able to make some progress toward her port.

The main yard, a heavy beam that in better days held a main sail aloft, had been lowered to the deck at the beginning of the storm. After analyzing the possibilities, it was decided that the beam should be used to replace the main mast that had been lost. The sailors lost no time in fitting it to the purpose and grafted it to the stump of the old mast, eight to ten feet above the deck.

It was hard to find rigging that could be used with this improvised mast, and after a topsail had been fitted to the purpose, there was nothing left for putting on more sail. The sea gradually grew smoother, and the weather more comfortable. For a while the company shook off despair as hope grew that they would survive the terrible journey.

Before long the shouts from aloft rang with news of another ship approaching. It was also bound for Virginia. With shouts from one ship to the other, they promised to stand by each other. The wind was north northwest when they tried to take latitude reading, always difficult in rough seas. Henry listened with great interest as the officers considered their calculations. At first they guessed that they were southward of Cape Hatteras. The first day the sun could clearly be seen at noon showed them the error. The current had carried the ship to the north beyond all their estimates. While they had thought they were south of the capes that mark the opening to the Chesapeake Bay, they had missed the entrance and had sailed north of the territory of Accomack. That, at least, was the strong opinion of Mate Putts, who was a well-respected sailor.

With a brisk wind pushing on improvised sails, the ship sped even faster than it had since they left Faial. Mate Putts, confidently affirmed that if the gale stood, they all would be dining the next day within the Capes. This was welcome news. The ship's water supply had long since been used. The meat was spoiled, and there was little left with which to feed the sorry company. Each man was allotted only a biscuit cake a day but even with that rationing there was not enough to last many days.

In the dark of the night as the ship tacked to gain the best use of the wind, they lost sight of the accompanying ship. Morning arrived in a fog, and the wind veered to the east hiding any clue of near land. According to the mate's computations, they were still well north of the capes. As the weather cleared, Putts climbed the mizzenmast to look about. Along the distant coastline small hills of pine trees were silhouetted against the sky. Putts pointed out certain hills as landmarks he had used in his twenty-two voyages to Virginia. With confidence in their direction, the sailors put on more sail as the growing daylight convinced the mate he was right.

All morning the ship lost sight of land and landmarks because of the dense fog. It was two or three in the afternoon by the time the sun and a northwest wind had cleared the coast of fog. When the land was again visible, Mate Putts didn't have to climb the mizzen to realize that he had been wrong in his earlier estimates of their position. He now realized there were similar landmarks south of the cape to those to the north, and it must have been the opening of the bay which made the land so far out of sight.

In the current state of the damaged ship, this was a serious matter. It would have been easy enough to change direction and easily remedy the mistake, had the sails and rigging been in any condition to hold a useful wind. Both Cape Henry and Cape Charles were nearly within their sight, but it was almost impossible to turn to the necessary direction. The whipstaff, a kind of lever, controlled a primitive rudder which was still operable, but most of the steering on a sailing vessel was accomplished by the set of the sails and with limited control over the improvised sails, the damaged ship was little better than a barge.

To uncomfortable passengers who had dreamed of sleeping in warm Virginia beds, this news was a bitter disappointment. Now the ship was again blown away from their goal in spite of everything that was tried to stop it. Sighs and groans were heard throughout the ship as they realized the remaining food would have to be stretched even farther. Half a biscuit cake a day was allotted to each man. The cakes were measured five to a pound, so a half cake was very little to live on. When the water ran low, the stock of Malaga sack was given plentifully to everyone but the strong white wine increased thirst rather than quenching it.

The gale that had caught them near the shore blew even stronger toward night and carried the ship off again at a great rate. Mate Putts agonized over his apparently fatal error in navigation and grew depressed. "We cherished him the best we could, and would not have him so profoundly sad, for what was rather his misfortune than his fault." said Norwood.

For many days and nights the ship was again pushed back into the heart of the ocean by an unrelenting northwest gale. It was estimated that the ship was at least a hundred leagues from the capes. From the time they had left Faial the ship had been battered and blown on the sea for more than forty days. The suffering of the passengers and crew increased every day. Finally the wind shifted to the east, but it was too gentle to be of much help in the rough seas that pushed against them, and the ship actually lost ground. In less than an hour the gale again shifted to the northwest. Again the ship was sent farther into the Atlantic terrifying the passengers with memories of the earlier storm.

Deep in the gloomy bowels of the ship, men took turns working the two pumps that bailed out the seas that washed in. One of the pumps broke down and could not be repaired. The other was kept going night and day, and no man was excused from his turn.

Among the serious perils that threatened the struggling ship was the state of the guns. The heavy cannon were on the rolling deck. Although tied in place, some of them broke because the tackle that held them had grown rotten. The ship rolled violently, especially when the sails were hauled down for repairs which was at least a third of the time.

To prevent a sure disaster if one of the guns were to get loose, Mate Putts had seamen place timbers over the hatchway stairs. With the assistance of a lucky stretch of smooth water the men were able to safely move the heavy guns below decks. There they helped by adding ballast to the center of the ship and removing the danger of a loose cannon on deck.

Even the most seasoned officers were unable to advise the best course to take. In less than a week's time the ship had been driven over two hundred leagues, but in what direction? Some reckoned the ship had made her way to the south and might be able to approach the Bermudas. Others argued that the winter season would make it difficult to find the islands before provisions were entirely gone.

The ship could not go back, and the winds were not accommodating to move it directly toward Virginia. At last the group agreed on a middle course. It was resolved that they would try to sail for the first American land that could be sighted, even if the ship was blown as far north as the coast of New England.

The growing famine increased the suffering of women and children whose cries could be heard throughout the ship. "The infinite number of rats that all the voyage had been our plague, we now were glad to make our prey to feed on" Norwood reported. "as they were ensnared and taken, a well grown rat was sold for sixteen shillings as a market rate.. Nay, before the voyage did end (as I was credibly informed) a woman great with child offered twenty shillings for a rat, which the proprietor refusing, the woman died."

Many sorrowful days and nights continued the bleak times until Christmas. To celebrate the day, scrapings of the meal tubs were all gathered to make a kind of pudding and mixed with Malaga sack, seawater, fruit and spice all fried in oil. The meager feast raised envy in some of those not invited to the captain's mess. Norwood and his friends, who were included, reported that they met with no actual resistance from the uninvited.

The lack of drinking water while surrounded by miles of ocean affected everyone equally. Norwood said "my dreams were all of cellars, and taps running down my throat, which made my waking much the worse by that tantalizing fancy." He was lucky in his friendship with the captain as he was allowed to share in some claret from the captain's private cellar. While it did little to quench the thirst, it was a sort of refreshment.

One day the captain singled Norwood out to go with him into the hold to look for fresh water in the bottom of the empty casks. With much effort they were able to get a little although it was too thick to be very palatable. As the pair sat each on a cask of Malaga, the captain decided to taste their contents. They both tasted and tasted again. Although they didn't drink a great deal it was enough to affect them both, although each in a different way.

While Norwood felt somewhat refreshed by the cordial, the captain fell into a depression. He felt the ship's disasters to be his own fault, he said. It was on his conscience that he had brought so many people into such misery. Surely the inevitable loss of all would be held to his account in the afterlife. He apologized to Norwood for having brought him and his friends to this end and then he burst into tears.

The younger man comforted the captain as well as he could and pointed out that it was a miracle that they had survived so far. "I comforted him the best I could, and told him, we must submit to the hand of God, and rely on his goodness, hoping, that the same Providence which had hitherto so miraculously preserved us, would still be continued in our favor till we were in safety." Soon the pair emerged from below decks and Norwood went back to his friends who had been wondering about his absence.

Although the westerly wind continued to shorten their way to shore, it was likely to be a distant part of the coast from their intended port. This did not change their resolution to sail for the first land. The hope of touching solid ground, no matter where, supported the company through hunger and thirst, toil and fatigue. For eight or nine more days and nights they continued to live on hope.

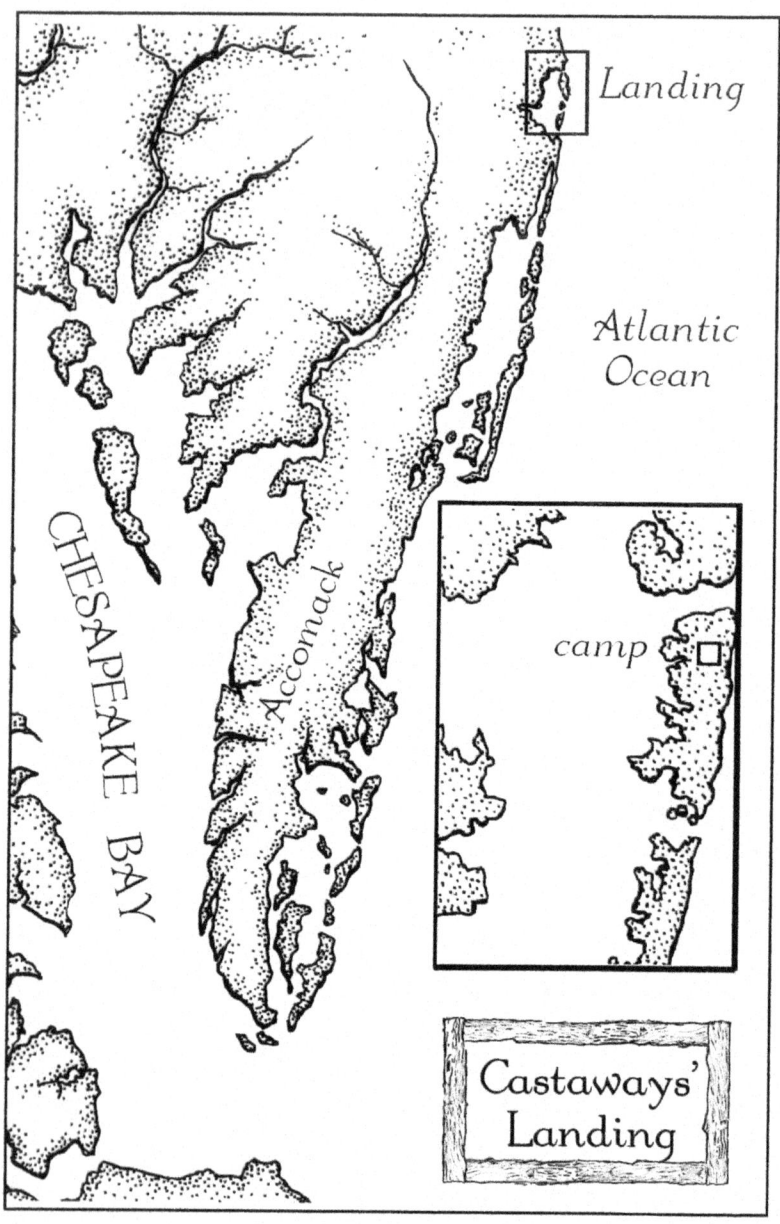

Four

Wilderness Landing

It was with great anticipation that they noted a change in the color of the water from the darker blue of deep ocean to the light blue near the coast. At last the ship approached the shore the night of January thirteenth. As morning lightened the sky they saw the land, but had no idea at what latitude.

The officers whose duty it was to keep the reckoning of the ship had totally given up that attempt. There had been no sun from which to take observations for many days, they said by way of excuse. The desperate state of the ship had made them careless about keeping a log or journal on a voyage they never expected to see end on land.

About three or four in the afternoon two days later the beleaguered *Virginia Merchant* at last drew close to the shores of the Americas. The weather was clear and everyone's spirits rose at their first sight of the coastline. They were about six or seven miles from shore and soundings said there were twenty-five fathoms of water with good ground for anchor-hold beneath them.

Dark forests were silhouetted against a pale winter sky. From time to time a whiff of cold pine-scented air drifted across the boat. Sailors said that in the heat of a summer afternoon it was possible to smell pines from the land even sixty miles out to sea. Everyone was excited by the proximity to solid land, and many wanted to go on shore at once.

The old officer who was in charge of the ship stores was against it. He was responsible for supplies and equipment on the ship while there were any, he said, and he would not consent to having the only remaining anchor out of his sight. He argued that the anchor could be lost if a sudden storm came upon them and that such a loss would be fatal. Without an anchor the ship would be at the mercy of any wind or tide and have no way to hold a position.

He also told them the ship's anchor cable was short and unfit to set the anchor safely in the open ocean. Not only that, the ship's crew was severely diminished by those who had died or been lost at sea. Passengers were weak and dying every day, and every possible person was needed to keep the pump going. Without constant bailing of the ship, it would soon be even less manageable and might yet sink.

Against the old man's reasoning, it was argued that the small remaining stock of biscuits would hardly hold a week. The entire ship was at risk if another northwestern storm were to come along and force it out to sea again. It seemed a likely possibility that a safe harbor was to be found in some coastal creek nearby.

These last reasons convinced the majority. When the anchor was at last dropped, Mate Putts was ordered to see what might be found on land. He took with him twelve of the sickest passengers who thought that they might find relief from their suffering on shore. Major Morrison went with them to see what could be learned from the land. He would be able to advise whether the ship should continue the voyage, or if it would be more prudent to land, unload the ship, and take their chances among the Indians. The group set off in the ship's only remaining small boat and rowed slowly toward the distant shoreline.

Four or five hours later those on the ship saw the boat returning with only Mate Putts in it. He was smiling broadly and full of good tidings. They had discovered a wide creek that would safely harbor the ship, he said. There was a depth of water sufficient for the ship to pass safely. Best of all, there was excellent fresh drinking water. Major Morrison sent some in a bottle for Norwood to sample. The shore was teeming with wildfowl which would be easy food for the starving company. The landing group had decided to stay on shore and wait for the others to join them. The news cheered everyone. Norwood expressed his interest in going immediately.

The captain was also in favor of the plan, hoping to save the lives of the passengers that remained. He embarked with Norwood in the wherry, along with a few others, so he could decide for himself the conditions that would be faced on land. The weary seamen were glad to have Norwood's help at the oars. On board ship, he had taken his turn at the pumps three or more hours a day; so he was hardened to the work. He commented that it was little effort to row the distance. "My passionate desires to be on shore at the fountainhead to drink without stint, did not a little quicken me, insomuch that the six or seven miles I rowed on this occasion, were no more than the breadth of the Thames at London at another time."

Winter's early darkness fell as they approached the shore, and they were glad to see the fires made by their friends in the distance. Not only were they welcome beacons to guide them; the fires were a great relief to warm them when they made landfall. The weather was intensely cold with a biting northwest wind. The coming night would be a bitter one.

As soon as the group landed, Major Morrison showed Norwood the running stream of water. He later related that he was so glad to be able to drink his fill of the fresh water that "I set my mouth against the stream that it might run into my thirsty stomach without stop. The rest of the company were at liberty to use their own methods to quench their thirst; but this I thought the greatest pleasure I ever enjoyed on earth."

After satisfying their thirst, the captain, Norwood, and a friend crossed the creek in the wherry, lured by the sounds of ducks and geese. The captain had a gun charged, and with the moon shining bright above them, he was able to kill a duck as the flock flew overhead. While the duck was being roasted on a stick by a seaman, the trio continued to walk along the shores of the creek to see what else could be found.

In passing a small gully they trod on an oyster bank and collected oysters to accompany the duck. Oysters attach themselves to rocks under water. In the wilds of a sandy shore they had built up shoals of oyster shells over thousands of years. Succeeding generations of oysters attached themselves to the shells of earlier ones to form a living bank of the mollusks. Beds of American Blue Point oysters are found all along the East coast. The Chesapeake Bay was known by the natives as the *Great Shellfish Bay*.

When the cooks had finished their work, the

Wilderness Landing 79

Castaway

group fell to the impromptu feast without the inconvenience of calling the rest of the company. Norwood comments that the small duck would have been little among so many and that "the fewer, the better cheer". It was agreed that the bones, head, legs and innards were to be the cook's fees. When the party finished, they returned to their friends "without making boast of our good fortunes."

The captain seemed satisfied by the depth of water in the creek. The ship could find safe harbor here. Toward daybreak he asked in Norwood's ear if he would go back with him to the ship. The reply was no. There would be no point, Norwood said, since the ship would be coming into the creek shortly, as had been agreed. Just before daybreak the captain reboarded the wherry to return to the ship. One of the captain's friends who was going back had a large coarse cape that Norwood borrowed to shelter him from the sharp cold.

The captain's small boat had well-cleared the shore heading back to the ship when the first light of dawn revealed a serious sight. "The first object we saw at sea was the ship under sail, standing for the capes with what canvas could be made to serve the turn. It was a very heavy prospect to us who remained (we knew not where) on shore, to see ourselves thus abandoned by the ship, and more, to be forsaken by the boat, so contrary to our mutual agreement."

It took many hours of tedious rowing for the captain to catch up with the *Virginia Merchant*. The seamen on board had set sail without the captain's order when the wind rose in a good direction to take them to the capes. Mate Putts, at his post on the mizzenmast saw the captain attempting to reach them and caused the ship to lay by until the captain was again on board.

There is no record of what transpired on the *Virginia Merchant* the rest of her voyage. There was no attempt to return to retrieve the abandoned passengers. It probably was not possible because of the ship's deteriorating condition. It took many days for the ship to make her way south to the mouth of the Chesapeake Bay and up the James River where it ran aground not far from her destination, the port at Jamestown.

Norwood, stood with the landing party on a cold windswept shore, "In this amazement and confusion of mind that no words can express, did our miserable distressed party condole with each other our being so cruelly abandoned in such a desolate place."

The sorrowful group first held prayers and then met to decide on a leader to direct their survival. Henry Norwood was the obvious choice. Then thirty-five years old, educated and well-bred, he was from a military background and accustomed to directing men and dealing with hardships. He was also energetic, strong, and one of the few who was entirely healthy.

They had little idea of their location except it was

many miles from civilization or hope of help. Norwood knew the general layout of the American coast from his reading, and suspected that they were somewhere between Virginia and the Dutch settlement at New Amsterdam, later called New York.

When he departed the ship for the land the evening before, Norwood left his servant, Thomas Harman, on board ship to look after his goods. In the bundle that Harman had packed for Norwood to take with him, was a cache of thirty biscuit cakes as he had advised his master.

Through weeks of starvation, the frugal Dutch servant had saved the biscuits from his own food allowance. As Norwood took over the task of leading the unhappy castaways on a cold beach, his first thought was of those cakes. He divided the bread into nineteen parts; the number of the party, and distributed the food as fairly as he could to the others, admitting to himself "perhaps I added the fraction to my own share."

It was about the sixteenth of January that they entered into life on land, "or rather into an orderly way unto our graves since nothing but the image of death was represented to us." The able-bodied men gathered together and those who knew how to use one were each assigned a fowling piece. Firearms of the period were difficult to handle and load and not particularly accurate.

A fowling piece fired a spray of small lead shot which reduced the need for accuracy. Francis Cary, a young gentleman with ambitions to be a Virginia planter, set off to lead the hunters. Norwood was glad to have Cary's assistance. "He was strong and healthy, and was very ready for any employment I could put upon him. He came recommended to me by Sir Edward Thurtan, his genius leading him rather to a planter's life abroad, than to any course his friends could propose to him in England and this rough entrance was like to let him know the worst at first." Francis Cary and his marksmen soon returned with some geese to feed the starving company.

As evening approached it was resolved that they could stay only one more night in those cold quarters and then must move farther inland. Norwood sent Cary up the creek to see what he might discover along the shore; "whether of Indians or any other living creatures that were likely to relieve our wants, or end our days."

The group prepared to die fighting like men if the natives were hostile or if peaceful they would be dealt with courtesy and a resolve to "please them with such trivial presents as they love to deal in, and so engage them into a friendship with us."

Cary set off along the inland shore but was not absent much above an hour when "we saw him return in a contrary point to that he sallied out upon. His face was clouded with the ill news he had to tell us, namely, that we were now residing on an island without any inhabitant, and that he had seen its whole extent, surrounded (as he believed) with water deeper than his head." He had not seen any natives or any other creatures except the ducks and geese flying overhead.

This news struck everyone into despair. Surely, they were all sentenced to a lingering death from hunger or cold. Norwood turned to find Cary had gone again. The younger man returned awhile later carrying a heavy burden; a parcel of oysters. He explained that he had hurt his feet on them as he crossed a small current of water. He had reached down and was able to feel with his hands what had caught at his feet. It took a great deal of pulling to loosen the oysters which were part of a large bank where they grew in heavy clusters.

While the January cold continued, great flocks of wildfowl came to the island. "Ducks and geese of all sorts some of every sort we killed and roasted on sticks, eating all but the feathers." As leader of the group, Norwood had the right of carving. He admits to "cutting the wing as large and full of meat as possible; whereas the rest was measured out as it were with scale and compass."

As the wind veered to the southward, the air grew a little warmer, but there were fewer fowl. "In their absence we were confined to the oyster bank, and a sort of weed some four inches long, and as thick as houseleek that was the only green (except pines) that the island afforded." It was nearly tasteless, but boiled with a little pepper that someone brought and five or six oysters, it became a grand meal.

The first night had been spent near the beach but was a miserable place to stay for any time. Besides the cold and windblown sand, the empty ocean lay as a constant reminder of their plight. Trapped on an isolated island, that wide expanse of water separated them from all they had ever known.

There was no hope that the *Virginia Merchant* might return, she might not make it to her destination. If by a miracle the ship did make it to Jamestown, there would be little reason to expect timely rescue from that quarter. If there were any sailors who would be able to direct a rescue ship, it would be weeks or months before the castaways could be found, if at all.

It was difficult to retain any semblance of hope but the group needed better quarters in which to spend the days and nights. Norwood and Cary explored the area to find a small clearing for their camp.

Behind the dunes there was a sparse forest of

Island Campfires

gnarled pines and scrubby undergrowth. The trees seemed to take up the middle of the island, where the ground was somewhat higher. The oceanside beaches lay to the east and the wide bay to the west.

Those who were well enough helped build makeshift shelters for the group, one for the women and another for the men. With the sound of wind moaning through the branches above them, they set to work.

Pine seemed to be the most common species of tree on the island. They collected branches and small trees and what undergrowth seemed useful. There were a few tools among the group but no one had the energy to spend cutting anything large in any case.

The womens hut was situated back in what seemed like a warmer spot. A shallow depression in the ground was built up a little on the sides. Using the pine branches and other materials, they overlapped the space like a tent. There were only three women so it was a small space, but the construction provided some protection from the wind. The women, who had been on their way to a new life in Virginia, had not fared well in the passage. All of them were weak from starvation and two of them could barely stand.

The shelter for men was similar to that for the women, but larger since there were more of them and it was impossible to make a roof over the whole. Several of the group had brought a few things with them from the ship, but no one had prepared for an extended stay without provisions.

The original plan had been for the ship to come in close to land and anchor in the nearby creek. Then there would have been access to additional supplies. What had seemed warm clothing when on the ship was inadequate to the winter damp on an inhospitable shore and now nothing more was available.

A fire was kept going to ward off animals and provide some warmth. Some dared to hope that perhaps the fire might also serve as a beacon to call for help. One morning as Norwood walked along the seaside with a long gun loaded with small shot, he fired at a flock of small birds called *oxeyes* and killed many of them. This provided a fine supper for the company.

The harvest came to an abrupt end a few days later as warming weather chased the fowl farther to the north. Although they had found food enough to keep them going while the wildfowl were frequent visitors, there was no dependable supply when the birds were gone. Having lived on scant rations for many weeks on the sea, the depressed group felt that they would surely die from famine. Each day was just a minor postponement of the inevitable.

The same southwest winds that carried away the fowl brought heavy rains which coincided with spring tides to flood the oyster bank. When the water finally receded to make the oysters again accessible, the weakened men could hardly pull them out of the muddy beds. At the same time, most of the guns were unworkable. The gunpowder had decayed from moisture. Oysters were the only available food, and after six days on the island most of the accessible oysters had been eaten.

"Of the three weak women, one had the envied happiness to die about this time" notes Norwood. "It was my advice to the survivors, who were following her apace, to endeavor their own preservation by converting her dead carcass into food, as they did to good effect." The men carried out the same advice as four died one bitter Sunday night a few days later.

What seems callous cannibalism from a modern viewpoint was a pragmatic and not uncommon solution for desperate travelers in the seventeenth century. Similar incidents had occurred in the Bermudas and other desolate areas after shipwrecks.

Norwood had seen maps of the region and felt sure they were stranded somewhere between Dutch territory to the north and settled lands of Virginia to the south. He does not mention Maryland in his account, although Lord Calvert established the colony at St Mary's City in 1634.

Perhaps he did not know of the new colony, or did not feel that Lord Baltimore's Catholic group had any claim to the Eastern Shore of the Chesapeake Bay. The land patents for both colonies were vaguely written, and disputes over borderlines persisted into the twentieth century. The island where Norwood's party was stranded is one of the barrier islands that now comprise Fenwick Island near the border of Maryland and Delaware.

The barrier islands are the shifting sands of the continental shelf and are frequently rearranged with the action of tides and storms. Until a canal was built later in the seventeenth century, the northern part of Fenwick Island was a peninsula. Just to the south the ocean had cut through to the Assawoman Bay in what the landing party had taken for a creek. Perhaps if they had made their inspection in full daylight they would have discovered their error in time. What is now a single long island, was at least three larger islands and many shoals and marshes 350 years ago.

When Norwood and the captain crossed the creek to do some moonlight duck shooting, they probably crossed north to the Fenwick side. After their feast, they returned to the rest of the group who were camped in the area that today is north Ocean City, Maryland.

In the cold wind-driven rain, the heaviest work fell on those who were strongest. Norwood labored to collect fuel for the fires that had to be kept going to preserve the group. As night approached, they moved into the meager shelter which they hoped would be some protection against a growing storm. Norwood spread a rough cape as a kind of tent against the winds. As many as could fit under it did so, while the rest managed for themselves.

A well-burning fire of two or three loads of wood and all the barrier they could arrange against the winds were little help against the bitterest cold any of them had ever known. Each man's clothes was singed and burnt on the side that faced the fire, while the side that was away from the fire was frozen. Those who lay near the flame could not stay long to enjoy the warmth, but were forced to move back to avoid suffocation by the smoke and flame. The crackling of the fire could not drown out the doleful sounds of the wind and the whipping of the pines overhead. Those who were able to sleep at all, slept fitfully.

When another day dawned to a cold and cloudy sky, the survivors met to discuss what could be done to spin out their lives a little longer. Norwood's friend, Major Morrison, on whose advice he most relied, was declining daily. He was very weak, and his legs could no longer support him. The Major was exhibiting symptoms of scurvy, caused by the lack of vitamin C and weeks of starvation. Norwood remained healthy and relatively strong, perhaps thanks to his avid enjoyment of Faial peaches. He considered that he alone was well enough to accomplish some form of rescue if it were decided how it could be done.

One of the group commented that it was the fact of their being on an island that was the biggest problem. The only proposal Norwood could think to make was to attempt to swim to the mainland, a distance of about a hundred yards. From there it would be possible to walk along the woods to the southwest which was the general direction of Virginia and a likely meeting a group of natives. "Indians would either relieve or destroy us. I fancied the former would be our lot when they should see our conditions, and that no hurt was intended to them, or if they should prove inhuman and of a bloody nature, and would not give us quarter, why even in that case it would be worth this labor of mine to procure a sudden period to all our miseries. "

One evening, around a comfortless fire, Norwood told the company about his idea to swim to the mainland. They were surprised that he intended to swim the icy water and make such a drastic attempt, but agreed that it was the only possible course of action to take. It was decided to try to arrange for provisions for the exhausting expedition. There was not much to choose from in the way of food. The oyster bank was all that could be relied on. They decided to stew enough oysters to fill two bottles and hope it would be enough to support the young man's travels.

It was about the ninth day of their residence on

the island when Cary went to collect the oysters, and Norwood set up to cook and bottle them for his provisions. He was working on his cookery when Cary brought word he had seen Indians on the mainland. Norwood ran to see for himself, but the Indians, if there had ever been any, were gone. Cary was young and imaginative, Norwood considered, and it was not the first false hope that had been raised.

Norwood returned to his work, disappointed in his hopes to see Indians without having to make the journey to seek them out. When the bottle was half full of oysters, he took a break to follow the sound of geese on the shore. Carefully, he approached the flock and was lucky enough to kill one. This goose he resolved to eat alone, deducting the head, bones and guts that were to be the cook's fees. After a good meal he would be better able to swim the creek and set on his journey, he reasoned.

He hung the goose on a crook of a tree and went to call aside the cook and ask him to bring a firebrand and a spit for roasting. When they returned to the place sometime later the goose was gone, except for the head. The body had been stolen by wolves which were common on the island, they later learned.

Norwood was greatly aggravated by the loss of the bird. "I wished I could have taken the thief of my goose to have served him in the same kind, and to have taken my revenge in the law of retaliation." What troubled him more was the thought that it was divine justice to have lost the goose when he had meant to eat it alone. As he thought about it further he decided that perhaps it was not a breach of trust. He intended only to gain enough strength to make his attempt to rescue the others.

While Norwood suffered his disappointment over losing the body of his goose, the cook had at least not lost his fee since the head and neck were still on the tree. Norwood returned to his oyster cookery. He had little confidence in the news that came from time to time of Indians seen on the other side of the creek, since he had not seen them himself.

The next morning as he was making final preparations for departure, one of the men came to say a canoe had been seen lying along the broken ground to the south of the island. This news Norwood again discounted as another mistake of imagination like all the others. But when he was told Indians had been to the women's cabin in the night and brought them shellfish to eat, he left immediately to hear the story from them directly. Both women swore it was the truth. Indians had come in the night and brought them food. They showed Norwood the shells, which were unlike any he had seen.

The women said that the Indians tried to communicate a message. They pointed to the southeast with their hands and made gestures difficult to interpret. The women said they thought it meant that the natives would come again tomorrow. It was reasoned their pointing to the southwest meant the time they would come, about nine o'clock, since that would be where the sun stood in the sky at that time.

Norwood knew from his reading that even if the women had understood the language of the natives, "they could not have learned the time of the day by any other computation than pointing at the sun. It is all the clock they have for the day, as the coming and going of the Cabuncks (the geese) is their almanac for the coming of winter and summer seasons."

Even in Europe mechanical clocks were rare in the seventeenth century although a church or important building might have one on a tower. Christian

Huygens' pendulum clock was not introduced until 1656, although Galileo is credited with the original design. Many country people probably had never seen a clock. Farmers and other laborers worked from sunrise to sunset with little or no more need of counting the hours than the Indians.

The news that friendly Indians had come to the island spread through the group of castaways. That the natives had brought food and would return, greatly relieved the weight of despair on the surviving company. "This news gave us all new life, almost working miracles amongst us, by making those who had desponded, and totally yielded themselves up to the weight of despair, and lay down with an intent never more to rise again, to take up their beds and walk."

This charitable visit of Indians put a stop to Norwood's preparations to swim the icy creek to seek them. A bitter wind was coming from the northwest. "So cold a gale was upon the surface of the water in the creek I was to pass, that in the general opinion of all the concerned, it was not a thing to be attempted; and that if I did, I must surely perish in the act. I was easily persuaded to forbear an action so dangerous because I believed the Indians would bring us off if our patience would hold out."

The group began to prepare for the coming meeting with the natives. Each able-bodied man was given a gun to lie by his side, laden with shot and in as good condition as possible. The guns would not be handled unless the natives presented a threat. If they came in a friendly posture, they would be met cheerfully and unarmed. The Indians were known to like happy faces.

Like many educated and curious Englishmen, Norwood had read Captain John Smith's books. Smith had thoroughly explored the Chesapeake Tidewater region in the early 1600s, and his adventures with the natives were legendary. His second book, A Map of Virginia, was published in 1612 and included detailed information on the natives including language and traditions. The Generall Historie of Virginia, New-England, and the Summer Isles, the largest and most influential of Smith's books, was published in 1623.

Smith's volumes included detailed maps of the area that were updated ten times and were still in general use forty years after they were printed. Much of what Norwood knew of the New World, he had read in Smith's informative books. In an era when books were expensive and rare, they were borrowed, traded and read many times. The printed word was treasured, and Smith's firsthand reports gave valuable details about the land and natives of Virginia.

As the morning sun rose and approached the southeast, every eye watched the woods to see the approach of the rescuers. When the sun reached the south, they thought they had been forgotten and began to fear the worst; that yet another misfortune would meet them.

Scouts were sent out to the north or south, but when noon approached with no sign of visitors, Norwood returned to his resolution of swimming to them. He felt it was the only possible course of action, but cold weather made it easy to postpone. The northerly wind was blowing too cold across the surface of the water that he would have to cross. His friends suggested that it was best not attempted. Norwood was easily persuaded to postpone the trip; partly because he believed the Indians would eventually arrive to save them.

Finally, at two or three o'clock in the afternoon, a

group of Indians came out from behind a large tree where they had been hiding. There were twenty or thirty men, women and children. The Englishmen were pleased to see that the natives held no weapons and all had cheerful faces. The natives shook hands and spoke to everyone they met with joyful smiles. The words *Ny Tops T'op* were often repeated and seemed to be a word that meant *friend*.

The natives were of small stature and wore skins of deer and beaver around their shoulders with the fur side against their skins. The long part hung down in the back like a cloak. Men and women wore a kind of apron decorated with shells or fringe. The legs and feet of men and women were wrapped in laced leather. The natives seemed to notice the cold less than the English, although they wore fewer coverings to protect them. From birth Indians bathed daily in streams or rivers and all year lived more outdoors than in.

After many greetings were exchanged, evening approached, and the group began trying to talk with each other. "We fell to parley with each other but performed it in signs more confounded and unintelligible than any other conversation I ever met withal, as hard to be interpreted as if they had expressed their thoughts in the Hebrew or Chaldean tongues." Norwood admitted.

The Indians immediately identified Norwood as leader of the group. He was not really surprised. "They did me the honor to make all applications to me, as being of largest dimensions, and equipped in a camlet coat glittering with galoon lace of gold and silver." Clothes make the man, or as Norwood wryly quotes, "where knowledge informs not, the habit qualifies." Camlet, a stiff fiber of camel hair and silk, was a fashionable material used in fine warm coats for gentlemen.

Norwood's coat may have been dyed blue as that was a color natives considered appropriate for royalty. Decorated with elegant metallic trim and shiny buttons, it was unlike anything the Indians had ever seen.

The Indians attempted to communicate with hand signs to augment their spoken language. The strange gestures and words were less intelligible than any language Norwood had ever encountered. He had no idea what they were trying to communicate, and they understood none of what he uttered or tried to express with hand signs and body motions. The Algonguian language spoken by the natives contained few consonants and the liquid sounds probably made it difficult to distinguish separate words.

There was no need to interpret the ears of Indian corn that were presented to the desperate castaways. It was also plain to see how the sight of so many starving strangers stirred the compassion of the native women.

One of the women gave Norwood the present of the leg of a swan. He thankfully accepted her gift and said "it was so much the more excellent, by how much it was larger than the greatest limb of any fowl I ever saw."

The Indians stayed on the island about two hours.

Island Meeting

Before they left they made a new appointment. They indicated by pointing to the sun that they would return about two o'clock in the afternoon the next day.

Norwood made an effort to gain their good will. "I made the chief of them presents of ribbon and other slight trade, which they loved, designing, by mutual endearment, to let them see, it would gratify their interest as well as their charity, to treat us well."

Some of the enterprising travelers had brought with them some of the small mirrors, colorful ribbons and beads that were known to be of value to the natives. Now they were glad to find them useful.

"Ha-na Haw", meaning farewell, was their parting word as the smiling natives again pointed at the place where the sun would be at their return. The survivors waved and returned the calls of "Ha-na Haw". It was hard for the weary troop to watch their new friends leaving them behind to spend another night on the desolate island but the food and hope the natives left behind were cause enough for rejoicing. The castaways were forced to be patient while they waited for transportation to arrive which would take them to the mainland.

The next day the Indians were late in arriving. "The delay of the Indians coming next day, beyond their set time, we thought an age of tedious years. "' At two o'clock there was no news. A little while later, a large number of Indian men, women, and children came around the huts with bread and corn for everyone. Many natives asked for beads and other little items as if in exchange for what they gave. While those who had such things gave them freely, those who had nothing to trade were given bread nonetheless.

An old man who seemed to be an elder of the native band tried to converse with Norwood. The Cavalier understood that the elder represented the king of Kickotank, whose territory included the island. The native seemed to want to learn something about why the group was there and in such a sorry state "I made return to him in many vain words, and in as many insignificant signs as himself had made to me, and neither of us one jot the wiser." As much as either side tried, neither could make himself understood to the other.

At last Norwood remembered reading something from John Smith's account of his travels among Indians along the Chesapeake. He recalled that the word *weroance*, which was one frequently repeated by the old man, meant king or leader. Norwood repeated the word to indicate that he understood the meaning. Using the word with strong emphasis and with gestures and motions, he tried to communicate the idea of wishing to go to the weroance of Kickotank.

This seemed to please the old native. He suddenly embraced the young man with great enthusiasm to express his joy at understanding. Norwood noted "This one word was all the Indian I could speak, which (like a little armor well placed) contributed to the saving of our lives."

The old man led Norwood to the water and a small canoe. A third man rowed the canoe south along the edge of the island to a marshy area. There they stopped at a place where a much larger canoe was pushed up against the bank. It was the same one that some of Norwood's group had seen there earlier. Once he saw the craft Norwood understood why the Indians had brought him. He was needed to help the two Indians launch the heavy boat and fetch it back to the group.

The larger canoe was about twenty-two feet long and made from a single tree trunk. Norwood described it as hollowed out "like a pig trough" and noted that it was very heavy for its proportion. The inside was black and charred, but smooth.

Native boat builders used fires to hollow out a suitable tree trunk. Patiently they smeared pitch, probably sap from the common pitch pine, on the wood. Then carefully they set fire to it, and little by little scraped away the charred wood with sharpened shells.

Although heavy and ungainly, the canoe provided serviceable transportation on calm water. Norwood describes the canoe as oak or pine but it was more likely bald cypress from the nearby swamps. The Englishman expressed surprise at the way in which the craft was propelled through the shallow water. "The laborers with long booms place their feet on the starboard and larboard sides of the boat and with this fickle footing do they heave it forward."

As the weary travelers assembled to go with the Indians, there was an hysterical outburst from one of the group. Major Stephens, who had been an officer in the Civil War, felt his rank gave him a right to be heard. He was vehemently against entering the canoes for the purpose of going with the Indians to see the king of Kickotank. He cried out loudly that the Indians would take them away only to kill them. He tried to persuade the group they should take the canoes forcibly from the Indians and make a run for the mouth of the Chesapeake.

Norwood and others tried to convince Major Stephens his fears were unreasonable. The idea of going to the Chesapeake in small canoes was ridiculous. They did not know the distance or directions to Virginia. He pointed out that they had been in the king's power since they set foot on that ground. If the king had wanted them dead, he would have ignored the castaways and let them starve to death or freeze on the island.

Native Transport

The consensus of the group was for going with the smiling Indians. Norwood noted that after the recent shipboard ordeal he would rather take his chance on the honor of a savage king than to the billows of the sea. There had been no indications at all that the natives were anything but peaceable and concerned for the welfare of the sorry band of strangers that had appeared among them and in such distress.

The worried Major Stephens continued with them, but repeated his fear of the natives on several occasions. Perhaps he was all too aware of the stories of murder, treachery, and torture by Indians that had been common along the James River earlier in the century.

While the canoes were being loaded, Norwood took a count of the group. There were thirteen, six less than the number that had came on shore; four men and two women. Five of the six were dead, but one living woman was missing. Through signs and pointing, Norwood expressed the missing woman's plight to the Indians. The natives indicated that she would be sought and would be cared for as soon as the rest were settled in new quarters.

The travelers at last left the island and were guided across an expanse of water until they entered a branch of the creek to the south. The tide was going out as they were slowly propelled along the creek by the Indians. Some of the hungry travelers treated themselves to oysters as they went; picking the mollusks out of the shallow water, cutting them open, devouring them, and disposing of the shells along the way.

Five

Native Hospitality

The canoes landed at the head of the southern creek branch. There the passengers were met by more smiling faces at the home of a native fisherman. They were invited to enter the native's home, a primitive hut set among the forest trees.

It was built with saplings stuck in the ground in two wide rows and lashed together overhead to create an arch. Branches and vines were tied horizontally to give strength to the rounded structure. Mats of woven reeds and grasses were attached to the framework and bark and moss provided insulation against the cold. The result was a long, rounded building that seemed more grown by nature than built by man. The doorway was a low opening in one end and protected from the wind by a flap.

Norwood was impressed by the simple beauty of the dwelling. "It had a loveliness and symmetry in the air of it, so pleasing to the eye and refreshing to the mind, that neither the splendor of the Escurial, or the glorious appearance of Versailles were able to stand in competition with it." The Escurial was a grand Spanish palace and Versailles the famous palace in France. Norwood was well traveled, but he had an appreciation for nature and simplicity.

Everyone stooped low to enter the small doorway and crowded inside the structure. Furs were given to the freezing visitors to fend off the cold. Several fires were laid in the center of the dwelling and small clay pots were set with their conical bases among the coals, boiling with what foods were available. Norwood, as the leader of this strange group, was treated as royalty.

He was given a large platform piled with furs and deerskins on which to rest. After suffering disaster at sea and deprivation on land, he was touched by the simple generosity of the natives who had saved them. He considered that their reception among the pagan savages seemed a strong contrast to the actions of Christians of certain English seacoasts who were known to attack, rob and even kill victims of shipwrecks rather than help them.

Norwood was touched by the poor fisherman's manner. "Our charitable host, influenced only by natural law, without the least show of coveting any thing we had, or prospect of reward in the future, did not only treat in this manner our persons, but did also, with as much honesty, secure for us our small stores of guns, powder as if he had read and understood the duty of the gospel or had given his only child as a hostage to secure his dealing justly with us."

The natives had no understanding of individual ownership of property in the European sense. In his world, tools or ornaments were used by whoever among his tribe needed them at the time and then handed to the next person who had use for them. Hospitality was an important part of the culture of the Algonquin tribes. "I cannot sufficiently applaud the humanity of this Indian, nor express the high contentment that I enjoyed in this poor man's cottage which was made of nothing but mat and reeds and bark of trees fixed to poles."

The travelers feasted on boiled swan, and, well-fed, settled to the first warm and comfortable night since their arrival in America. The next morning dawned crisp and sunny. After a plentiful breakfast, they prepared to go on to where the king of Kickotank resided.

The woman left behind at the island had been found and reunited with her traveling companion. Neither of the two women was in any condition for a journey, however. They remained to be carefully nourished and attended at the fisherman's house until a boat came to take them to Virginia several months later. Norwood remarked that the pair arrived eventually in Jamestown in perfect health and one or both of them married and raised families in Virginia.

The remaining group began their journey through the thick woods. They had not gone half a mile when they heard a noise of men's voices behind them, seeming to call for them to stop. Several Indians had been sent by the king to order them back to their quarters. In confusion, they turned around. Major Stephens became very alarmed. He was convinced the Indian king had changed his mind and had sent these men to torture and kill them all. The Major's agitation was quieted by the group who seemed satisfied with Norwood's leadership.

There seemed to be no reason to suspect such a change of heart from the Indians who had so kindly helped them. The natives who came and called to them were all unarmed. When the English group returned to the creek, it was made plain that the king had been told of the visitors' weak condition and understood that it would be a hardship for them to walk the four miles through the woods to his house. He had sent canoes to carry the

Queen's Welcome

travelers along another branch of the same creek to a place which was nearest to his house.

The canoes lay ready on the creek bank. In the bright winter sunshine, the visitors had a pleasant passage along the shallow creek, again eating oysters all the way. Norwood notes that although they had all eaten a large breakfast a short time before, they had been getting along on scant rations for many weeks and there was a lot of catching up to do. The "arrears to our stomachs was so great, that all we swallowed was soon concocted, and our appetite still fresh and craving more."

Indians poled the canoes about three miles along another branch of the creek. They landed near the house of a queen "then in waiting" (pregnant) of that territory. Norwood describes her as a plain-looking lady who was not young or misshapen, but with a complexion of a "sad white" which seemed unhealthy when contrasted with younger, more tawny natives.

As did any of his contemporaries, Norwood tried to understand the natives he met in European terms. John

Smith had described the word *weroance* as a king or war leader who ruled a kingdom or territory. The king of Kickotank was indeed an hereditary ruler of a group, but it was more likely an extended family. His kingdom was not a territory he owned, but a family hunting area. Indians had no understanding of the ownership of property, especially land. To the natives, the forests, fields and waterways were part of Mother Earth who fed her people with the bounty of corn, game and other wild foods.

The Algonquian language had many dialects. Even tribes that lived near each other did not always understand their neighbors. The hand gestures that were so incomprehensible to Norwood were the universal language that tribes used to make themselves understood.

Norwood refers to the *king* of Kickotank but he did not indicate if that was the name of the people, the leader or the place of his house. Often the Indians did not understand what was being asked when they were questioned about names or places. In many cases, descriptive Indian phrases were used by the English incorrectly. Indians did not generalize with their names. A native phrase that described a particular camping spot might be used by the English as a name for whole river nearby.

There are several unrelated occurrences of the name Kickotank or Kegotank on the Eastern Shore of Maryland and Virginia. No exact translation of the name survives but *tank* indicates a neck of water. It seems likely that Kickotank referred to the area or the place of the king's residence that particular winter. Since Indians moved frequently, no village or home was considered permanent.

The primitive farming methods they used made it necessary to move or extend the fields almost constantly.

They would *girdle* or strip the bark from trees, causing them to die. Corn, squash and other crops were planted in the area while the trees stood with leafless branches letting in the sunlight. Sometimes the dead trees were cut down, but without metal axes the process was tedious and not really necessary. Women planted and cared for the crops and small children kept birds away. A field would be planted for several years but without fertilizers the thin soil was soon depleted. Then it would be necessary to find and clear another field, leaving the former one to grow wild with blackberries and brambles, making homes for rabbits and other small game.

In winter the natives dispersed their group and set up their mat-covered houses over a wide area to take advantage of a variable winter food supply. After autumn harvests feasts, the Indians were fatter. The extra layer provided warmth and insurance against lean times at the end of a long winter.

The people of Kickotank that Norwood met apparently lived without fear of attack from enemies. They had no stockade fences around their homes or farms. Located as they were on the Atlantic seaboard, they were isolated enough not to have felt pressure from English settlers or attacks from warlike Susquehanna Indians to the north.

A mat was spread outside on the ground in front of the queen's house. Pone, a kind of bread made from corn and fat and cooked on heated stones, was set before the hungry visitors, along with hominy, oysters, and meats. The queen invited the guests to sit down and eat.

"Her gestures showed more of courtesy than majesty", Norwood remarked, as he compared the Indian woman with the great ladies he had known. The Cavalier had met elegant and highborn women in Europe and knew in her own society, the native woman was royalty.

The woman's plain features and simple leather clothing were a strong contrast to the silk, lace and jewels of European ladies, but he admired the native's kindness and the courtesy she showed her guests. "The beauty of this queen's mind (which is more permanent than that of color) was conspicuous in her charity and generosity to us poor starved weather-beaten creatures, who were the object of it."

Since they had left the island the southerly winds made for mild weather, but it did not appear that it would last long. A northwest gale soon threatened to bring another storm, and the group was anxious to find shelter before the rain or snow came down on them. When the meal with the queen was finished, Norwood took formal leave from her with all the show of gratitude that he could manage without a common language between them.

The group set off on a half hour's walk to the king's lodging. Although Norwood had read of John Smith's adventures with the natives of the Chesapeake area, the young Cavalier had only a general idea of Indian culture. He expected the king's palace to be more elegant or constructed of better materials than the house of a common citizen, but he was disappointed.

The native guides pointed out the king's home by the smoke rising from it. The oval house was made of the same materials as the other dwellings they already had visited. It was built of locust posts sunk in the ground at the corners and partitions. These posts gave support to the mats and reeds that were attached to it. Overhead, the posts met to support the roof, which was tied to the body of the house with rushes.

The king's house was a little longer than most of the others in the small village. It was about eighteen or twenty feet wide and sixty feet long. Even inside, it was not the palace the Cavalier imagined it would be. The only furniture consisted of several platforms, each about six to eight feet long, set on both sides of the long house and separated by a space of about five feet in the middle. In this space were many fires all burning at once.

Norwood counted fourteen fires, each sending smoke upward to a hole in the roof above each fireplace. Most of the smoke remained in the building however, swirling around people sitting on the platforms on either side of the fires. The king did have a platform that was twice as long as the rest. It was lavishly laid with finely dressed deerskins and the best otter and beaver furs.

The guests were shown to an area of their own with a warm fire where they were left to rest for a while. When the king was ready to meet his guests, he sent his daughter to them. The pretty girl of about ten or twelve years old brought in a large wooden bowl full of hominy, which is corn, beaten and boiled into a thick mash. Dried corn, served as pone or hominy, was the natives' staple food for winter. Even the name hominy is from the Algonquian word *rockahominie* meaning parched corn.

The maiden went first to Norwood with the bowl. "She did in a most obliging manner give me the first taste of it, which I would have handed to my next neighbor

Native Village

after I had eaten, but the young princess interposed her hand, and taking the bowl out of mine, delivered it to the same party I aimed to give it, and so to all the rest of us in order." Each visitor was ceremoniously presented with the bowl of hominy in turn, and each ate from it using a mussel shell for a spoon.

At the end of this formal offering of food, the guests were presented with a means of washing themselves. Norwood remarks that "The linen of that country grows ready-made on the branches of oak trees or pine. The English call it moss. It is like the threads of uncured cotton-yarn raveled, and hangs in parcels on the lower boughs, divine providence having so ordered it for the convenience and sustenance of the deer, which is all the food they can get in times of snow. It is very soft, sweet and cleanly, and fit for the purpose of keeping clean the hands, and doing the duty of napkins."

This mention of what would later be called Spanish moss is curious. The plant is now extremely rare on the Delmarva peninsula, and unheard of so far north. Perhaps the Indians traded for the commodity from natives to the south. In the twentieth century Spanish moss has only been sighted occasionally at the southern tip of the peninsula. It may be that Norwood was mistaken about the source of the material. The soft sphagnum moss that grows abundantly in the nearby swamps looks similar to Spanish moss when dried. Sphagnum moss was used extensively by the natives for baby diapers and toweling, since it is very absorbent.

About three hours after this meal had ended, the king sent for Norwood to come to him. "He called me *Ny a Mutt* which is to say, *My brother*, and compelled me to sit down on the same bank with himself, which I had reason to look upon as a mighty favour." The king and his council, called *crotemen*, were having some kind of debate. The discussion was obviously about this group of strangers, who they were, how they had come there, and why they were in such a sad state.

The king addressed Norwood with many gestures and movements; his arms in various positions as if to explain what he could not say with a spoken language. Although the motions were universal signs among the natives, the gestures were totally meaningless to Norwood and he had no idea what the Indians were trying to say.

It frustrated Norwood to be unable to answer the questions put to him by the king, or to explain why the pathetic group was to be found on the desolate island in midwinter. Norwood tried to show that he would answer if he could and that he was distressed not to be able to understand the natives. When the king saw the young man's troubled face, he turned the conversation to joking and laughter and would not stop until he had made Norwood laugh with him. The abrupt change in his host's demeanor puzzled Norwood, who did not understand that the Indians valued good cheer with guests. A frowning guest indicated a poor host.

Since it was their first formal meeting, Norwood took the occasion to present the king with a sword and long shoulder belt. The king received them kindly. To show his appreciation, he took off the leather cloak that covered his shoulders and stood up on his platform while the young man dressed him with the gift. The king had nothing on except a brief leather loincloth and was quite delighted with the effect of harness and sword on his almost naked person. Norwood was struck with the absurdness of the picture, and it was not long before he was laughing in earnest.

After making this first short acquaintance with

the king, Norwood took his leave and returned to his comrades. As he moved between the fires he noticed one space was partitioned off with matting. He heard a sound from that area, a pounding "like the beating of hemp". He took it to be some sort of work space. Standing on tiptoe, he was able to peer in the small room and the view disturbed him. The same queen he had visited at first was hard at work beating the corn for the king's dinner.

In Norwood's experience royalty did not do servile labor, certainly not pounding corn between two rocks for a husband's dinner. He learned later that native women feel it a privilege to prepare and serve food for their husbands. The Indians would be as unwilling to give up that occupation as a Christian queen would be to do it, Norwood was told.

Several of the more important Indians followed Norwood back to his quarters. They used their best efforts to try to gain some understanding of the strangers who seemed to have been dropped from the sky. In their turn, the castaways were unable to make their hosts understand what had happened and why they were there. "They sought many ways to make their thoughts intelligible to us but still we parted without knowing what to fix upon, or how to steer our course in advance of our way to Virginia."

As they relaxed, warm and well-fed, the group discussed what was to be done next. They hoped, after regaining some of their strength through the generosity of the natives, they would be able to continue their travels over land. They must find a way to explain that they wanted to go to Virginia.

As the travelers grew healthier they grew more eager to continue to their destination. Norwood may have felt torn between his responsibilities as leader for the castaways and the pressures of time. He carried a letter of introduction from King Charles to Governor Berkeley, and it is likely he also was entrusted with other letters and documents from the exiled king or his deputies to the government in Virginia.

Norwood knew the importance of time in the current political situation. Charles II was a landless king with dwindling resources while Parliament was growing stronger on heavy taxation. The American colonies were important to both sides. Virginia had so far remained Royalist and sent tax money to Charles instead of Cromwell while Puritans in New England had sided with Parliament.

King Charles was counting on his Virginian supporters. The colony was prosperous from the tobacco trade and many landowners held land grants from the king. Money from wealthy Cavaliers would buy weapons as well as provide living expenses for the exiled monarch. The king may have sent the trusted Norwood to collect donations for his cause, or to give instructions important to the war effort. Resting in the dim interior of a remote native village, Norwood felt he had been away from civilization too long, and that he was needed elsewhere. He had received no news since leaving England in September and it was nearing February and he had not yet made it to his destination at Jamestown.

While the castaways were not yet able to continue their travels, they were recovering their strength thanks to the generosity of the natives. One morning the same pretty maiden came to the group and presented them a new food. It was a thick pudding about the color of almonds with a similar nutty taste. Norwood was surprised to learn it was made of dry hickory nuts, probably pignut hickory, which is common in the area. The thick-

Native Foods

shelled nut has a sweet kernel inside. A native demonstrated that the nuts were beaten in a mortar, shells and all, until reduced to a powder. Then the mixture was put in a tray and hollowed in the middle to make a place for water. As soon as the water was poured on the powder, it rose, white and creamy and after fermenting it took on the taste of the sweet nut. The natives often used nuts for flavoring their food and this dish was considered a special delicacy.

Major Morrison, who had been almost at death's door from starvation, especially enjoyed this unusual breakfast food. He wished the bowl had been a fathom deep, he asserted. If this princess would give him his fill of that wonderful food, he should soon recover his strength, the Major said.

As the travelers' bodies grew stronger, so grew their courage. The group discussed their plans around the Indians' fire. As many as were able would try to find a way to Virginia, they decided. They guessed it could not be a great distance from their location and was likely to be south by west to southwest to the Eastern Shore of Virginia. There was no way for them to determine the latitude. This discouraged them. They were confident from what the seamen said that they were south of the Menados, then a Dutch plantation and later New York.

"Fair weather and full stomachs made us willing to be gone." Explained Norwood. They began to put aside food for an expedition southward.

They would need a guide and resolved to recruit an Indian to lead them through the wilderness. It was known there were swamps and creeks all along the coasts and an informed guide would be vital to their success.

The king noticed their activity and remarked on the extra bread needed for the guests. He realized that the strangers planned to soon leave him and go off on their own. The king made use of all the gestures and pantomimes he could imagine to convince them of the difficulty of the trip.

Norwood was beginning to understand the ideas behind native language and gestures. "He showed us the danger we should expose ourselves unto, by rain and cold, swamps and darkness, unless, we were conducted by other skill than we could pretend to. He pointed to his fires and stocks of corn of which he had enough, and made it legible to us in his countenance that we were welcome to it."

There was still no way to communicate directly with the natives, but the king managed to make himself fully understood at this occasion. Norwood and his party retired to their quarters for another day.

Around midnight the following night, the king sent for Norwood. He was invited to sit next to him on the royal platform as before. Then the king showed Norwood the hindquarters of a lean doe that had just been brought in. He handed Norwood a knife to cut off whatever part he would have of it. Then he pointed to the fire, and the guest understood that he was to cook the piece himself.

"I could not readily tell how to show my skill in the cookery of it, with no better ingredients then appeared in sight and so did no more but cut a collop and cast it on the coals." The king laughed and showed him a better way.

The Indian put the meat on a long skewer and put the sharp end into the ground so that the meat was set at an angle over the fire. Turning sometimes one side and then the other to the heat, the meat was soon broiled and ready to eat. Norwood offered the meat first to the king and then to the nobles, but all refused, leaving the meal to the guest. The rest of the doe was cut in pieces and stewed in a clay pot. When it was cooked, it was given to Norwood to send to his comrades.

After the midnight dinner the king was determined to explain, through gestures and pantomime, how they capture a deer in the winter, especially when the ground is covered with snow. He showed Norwood a small leather thong in which he said that any kind of deer could be taken. Norwood could not fully understand how the leather trap was constructed, but he did understand its general use.

The Indians fastened a green pine branch to the end of a pole with a string so the green dangled down. and rested on his hind legs. When the animal pulled at the branch, it acted like a trigger and the trap closed. The animal was pulled up by its hind legs "his heels are struck up in the air, and there he remains on his back so straightly hampered, that the least child may approach to touch and take him." the Englishman was told.

After the demonstration, the king again tried to be understood. After three or four days in the native village, Norwood could better understand what was being communicated by the expression and gestures of the speaker more than the words. The king questioned whether the strangers wanted to go north or south. Norwood pointed to the south. At this the king seemed pleased. One of the king's crotemen, stepped up and gained his attention. He picked up a stick and made several circles in the dirt near the fire. Holding up a finger to make his point, he gave every circle a name. It was not hard for Norwood to understand that the Indian was showing him a map of the area to the south. The circle farthest south he called *Accawmacke*. Although the native pronounced it with an accent that differed from the English, Norwood knew the place and his face lit up. "I laid hold on that word with all demonstrations of satisfaction I could express, giving them to understand that was the place which we had a desire to be conducted."

There were joyful smiles all around when it was plain that the map was understood and that Accomack, was the place that the travelers wanted to go. When the English arrived in the Chesapeake Bay region, the natives referred to the Eastern Shore as the "across the water place" *Accawmacke*. Although separated from the mainland by the expanse of the Chesapeake Bay, it was one of the earliest areas of Virginia to be colonized and communication was frequent between settlers on the two shores. The tidewaters of the Chesapeake Bay were major highways in the seventeenth century. Sloops and ships frequently made the trip across the bay for trade, government business or social occasions.

The king was delighted that the stranger was pleased with this knowledge of their whereabouts. "He called a young man to him and seemed to give him instructions to do something for us" Norwood noted, "but what it was we were not yet able to resolve."

After two or three more days, the group again began to despair of setting out for the south before spring. Once again the king noticed that the strangers were planning to leave him. "He showed in his looks a more than ordinary resentment, still describing (as he could) the care he had taken for us, and impossibility of accomplishing our ends by ourselves." He seemed to say they would surely faint on the way or die without help if they went against his advice.

Once again he showed them his store of corn and made gestures that with his smiling face expressed that they would have plenty to eat if they would stay until he gave the word. As often as the travelers pointed or looked toward Accomack, the king shook his head and made grimaces that showed his disapproval of the plan until he approved it.

Norwood agreed. "I was abundantly convinced of our folly in the resolution we were ready to take of going away without better informaion of the distance from Accomack, and way that led to it. In the Indian village they had a fine welcome, and he, for one, was resolved to stay until the king approved the departure. It was becoming clear a messenger had been sent to Accomac on Norwood's behalf, and that the king waited for the messenger's return.

Indian Map

While the group lived in suspense waiting for the messenger to return from the south, the king asked to see their firearms. Several pieces were still in working order after their stay on the island. Many of the men had spent their time working to refurbish the guns during their recovery in the Indian village.

Norwood presented to the king the firearm the Indian most admired. The Cavalier showed the native king how to load the gun and fire it. The Indian was very shy at first, fearing that this formidable weapon might hurt him. Norwood showed the king how he should stand with the weapon, and since they were inside the house, he indicated for the king to point the gun out the chimney hole above them.

A shot echoed through the Indian village when the king fired the weapon. A flash of light in the mat and reed dwelling reminded Norwood that he had forgotten the combustible nature of the building material. At the shot, the flashing of the powder caught the edge of the smoke hole in the roof which instantly burst into flame. Immediately, one or two small boys nimbly scrambled up the oak boughs that held the walls and roof. Using their knives, they cut out the burning material and dropped it into the fire beneath. In a very few minutes the fire was put out, with little damage to the building to everyone's relief.

The king's eldest son who was about eighteen years old, was hugely enamored with the firearms after Norwood's demonstration. "He looked so wistfully on me when he saw what wonders they would do that I could not forbear presenting him with a birding piece."

Some of the company reminded Norwood that the laws of Virginia made it a criminal act to furnish Indians with firearms. He countered their arguments by saying while the law might be a good one in general but "as our condition was, I esteemed it a much greater crime to deny those Indians any thing that was in our power to give them." With his advantages of social position and kinship with Governor Berkeley, Norwood was not concerned with the penalties of a distant government. If he chose to reward their rescuers, he would give them whatever they wanted, he said.

  The native king of Kickotank obviously thought the strange weapon repaid him well for the costs of entertaining these unusual guests. His son was delighted, as well. Norwood took the young man outside to show him how to shoot at wildfowl. Carefully he showed the boy how to charge his gun and clean it. The birding piece fired small pellets like a shotgun so marksmanship was not so important. After a few minutes of demonstration the young Indian went out proudly carrying his new weapon. He crept up on a flock of geese in the nearby field. By firing at random, he managed to bring one of them down. When the young man returned, his game in his hand, it was with such a beaming attitude of pride it was "as if he had borrowed wings of the wind," Norwood recalled.

  Time passed slowly in the quiet Indian village. January closed and February began and the Englishmen all continued to wait, if somewhat impatiently, for the messenger's return. One afternoon near three o'clock the king made one of his visits to the guests' quarters and again singled Norwood out.

  The Cavalier felt sure it was not his own importance that was the reason for the king's frequent attentions; rather that his clothing was fancier than the rest of the company. The coat that Norwood wore, although old and worn, still glittered with ornate gold and silver lace cording and fancy buttons. Even singed and threadbare, the Cavalier fashions, commonplace in the courts of Europe, stood out against the rustic background of an Indian village.

The native king indicated that he thought the visitor appeared too melancholy. The Indians, disapproved of a sad expression, especially on a guest. Perhaps the years of Civil War and political conflict showed too plainly on Norwood's face, or the responsibilities of the present weighed heavily on the thirty-five year old man's shoulders. The king had noticed Norwood's depression, and he tried to show the younger man that he would rather have his visitor also smiling. The Indians had arranged a distraction for their favored guest, he indicated. His daughter came forward and the king gestured that Norwood was to go with her and follow her wherever she would go.

The surviving company watching the pantomime included Major Stephens. He still harbored a deep suspicion of the Indians and voiced his objections to Norwood's leaving the group. It was a trick, he argued, for the king to separate them. He suggested that when Norwood had been lured to a dark part of the forest he would be killed. The fear was so irrational that Norwood didn't want to respond to it. "I am honored that you are so concerned over my welfare," Norwood finally told Stephens. The absurd argument was turned to ridicule by the rest of the company.

In his account of his adventures, Norwood writes that the incidents concerning Major Stephens could very well have been omitted. It was not worthy of mention, he admits, but Stephens' "bad habits on shore were scandalously vicious, his mouth always belching oaths" He would have left out the mention of the man's behavior if Stephens had not been such a disagreeable bully. It was confirmation "that true innate courage does seldom reside in the heart of a quarrelling and talking hector."

The Cavalier had no qualms about agreeing to the king's direction. The winter evening was fast approaching as Norwood said goodbye to the other Englishmen and followed the Indian girl through the woods. It was another extremely cold night with a heavy frost and a bitter wind. "The winds blowing very fresh upon my face, it almost stopped my breath." Norwood recalled. He had spent the day under a warm roof with great fires filling the space with thick smoke. Once outdoors he suffered the north wind more by contrast.

Explorers along the Atlantic coast often noted the icy winds that come from the northwest, especially in winter. To Norwood's generation, the cause was obvious; "the mighty towering mountains to the northwest covered all the year with snow ... does refrigerate the air."

They presumed that the North American continent had mountains at its heart. The gentle Appalachian mountains that some explorers had seen to the west must be the edge of a massive range of mountains to rival the Alps, they assumed.

In less than a half hour the pain of walking in the bitter wind was over, the Cavalier and the Indian girl were in sight of the small house that was their goal. The lady of the house, who was the mother of Norwood's young guide, was there to meet them. Presumably this lady was another of the king's several wives. In the native culture a man could marry as many wives as he could afford, but the women kept their own homes.

This house was the same as the others Norwood had visited. He was shown to an area in the center where he was invited to relax on a platform. A rousing fire had been prepared to warm the traveler. Soon he was offered a feast. Wild turkey was boiled with oysters and stewed mussels into a meal Norwood heartily enjoyed. "It would have passed for a delicacy at any great table in England by palates more competent to make a judgment than mine," he said. He was "now more gratified with the quantity than the quality of what was before me."

This queen was much like the first lady they met at their landing place. Norwood subtly mentions that she was not what he expected in a queen. She was "somewhat ancient in proportion to the king's age, but so gentle and compassionate, as did very bountifully requite all defects of nature." In a society where the average life expectancy was not much more than thirty years, an individual was considered elderly at forty. The diet of stone ground corn caused wear on teeth and decay and tooth loss were common in the natives. She may not have been much older than her thirty-five year old visitor.

The lady sat for some hours at the fire with her guest. She was obviously curious about how and why the visitors had mysteriously appeared among them. Apparently the natives had not seen the ship, *Virginia Merchant*. For all the Indians knew, the group might have been spirited to the island by strange powers. Using pantomime and gestures Norwood tried to explain his adventures to the woman.

Although they talked for several hours, Norwood realized from the expression of his Indian hostess that she understood no more of his explanation than had the king. About nine o'clock everyone retired to bed. Since the longhouse was divided into compartments by screens of reed matting, each resident and guest was provided with privacy.

As soon as the sun was up, Norwood stepped outside and felt the same cold and icy northwest wind as the day before. He was glad to go back to the warm hospitality of the lady's smile and a good breakfast of stewed mussels. As he was eating, his young guide came in with orders from her father that the guest was to return as soon as possible. The messenger had returned from Accomack.

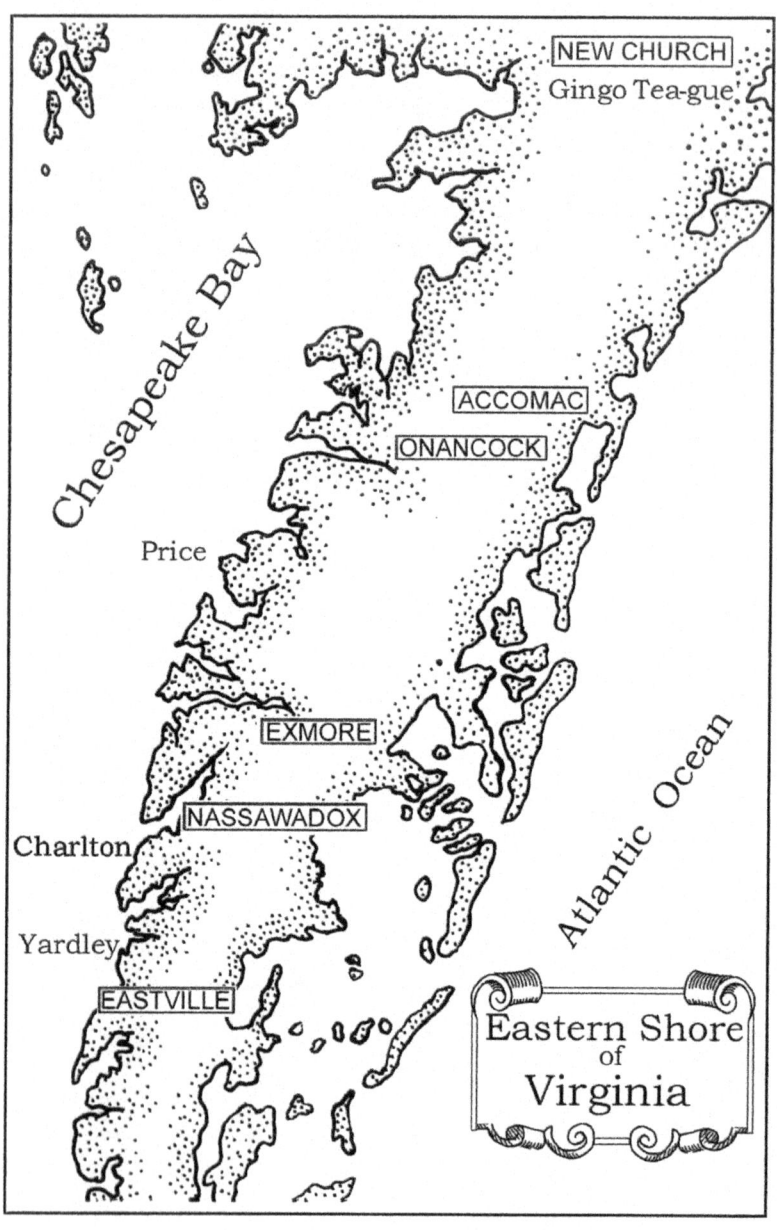

Six

Southern Expedition

Immediately after breakfast, the two retraced their steps back to the king of Kickotank's house. They hurried as much from the bitter cold as from their enthusiasm to return. "Nothing but a violent motion could make our limbs useful," Norwood recollected.

No sooner had he set foot in the longhouse than he could see the change on every face. Everyone was excited and spoke at once, telling him messengers had arrived and were now with the king. Norwood immediately hastened to meet them.

He spoke with one man he saw who was dressed in English clothes. The man introduced himself as Jenkin Price and that his business was to trade for furs. He had come with the guide who was the Kickotank Indian who had been sent south by the king.

Norwood told him his name and explained what had happened to his party and how they had been rescued by the natives.

Price said that word had been sent to the Eastern Shore from Governor Berkeley in Jamestown about the lost group. He wanted to find those who had been left behind when the ship went off without them. None of the colonists in Accomack had heard of the ship or knew where to find the lost company until the Indian brought the news from Kickotank.

Jenkin Price was able to give an account of the last leg of the voyage of the *Virginia Merchant*. After leaving the castaways, the ship had encountered even more dangers and difficulties as it struggled to maneuver into the Chesapeake Bay, he told them. She had limped into the James River only to run aground not far from her destination. The rest of the ship's passengers and all their goods were now safely in Jamestown.

Price had brought an Indian of his own area to act as a guide. The Indian, Jack, was from a tribe farther south. He was well acquainted with the trails through the swamps and forests back to Accomack, the colonist told Norwood. The king of Kickotank was glad to see the Cavalier's evident pleasure at meeting the trader.

The king was also pleased to have a chance to learn the guest's story through an interpreter. He had not been able to understand very much from the gestures and pantomimes the king and the Cavalier had so far used between them. Jenkin Price knew some of the Indian language, and Jack had learned some English on the plantations. Little by little Norwood explained his story to Price who translated for Jack who then explained the meaning to the king of Kickotank.

Unknown to Norwood, Jack added his own comments to the explanations. He told the king of the power and importance of the English in Virginia. He cautioned the natives not to embezzle any goods that the group had brought for fear of terrible justice from them. Norwood wondered what Jack was saying to the king as the Indians came in to stack up guns and other gifts to be returned to the English.

"I was very much ashamed of Jack's too great zeal in our service," Norwood recalled with dismay. The Indians had saved all of their lives, and he would have given them any reward for their generosity. Norwood carefully explained to the king that he had no part in what Jack had said and he made sure all the gifts were returned to the natives. Norwood was pleased to finally have even this imperfect method of communication with the king, however, and their friendship grew.

During the discussions Norwood finally began to picture their location. According to the Indians they were about fifty English miles from Virginia. It was a very rough measurement of the traditional native trail that wound southward down the center of the peninsula.

Jenkin Price was from Littleton's Plantation, the farthest north of the Virginia settlements on the east side of the Chesapeake Bay. Price encouraged Norwood to make the long walk back with him. "He gave me great encouragement to endure the length of the way by assuring me I should find neither stone or shrub to hurt my feet through my thin-soled boots for the whole colony had neither stone nor underwood." The Indian, Jack, was an excellent guide in the woods, Price assured the group. Since he was born in the area, he knew it well. Norwood agreed with the company those who were able would set out as soon as possible for Virginia.

The king did not want them to leave until the weather was somewhat milder. The travelers were still recovering from starvation and exposure, and this fact worried him. When he saw that the visitors were packing their goods and planning to go the next morning, he was disappointed. He had planned to entertain them all with a festival dance before they left. Most of the group would have put off the march a day or so longer in order to see the Indian celebration, but Norwood was set in his determination to be in gone as soon as possible. "I was wholly bent for Accomack, to which place I was to dance almost my bare feet, the thoughts of which took off the edge I might otherwise have had to novelties of that kind."

As a pledge of their friendship and brotherhood, the king asked if Norwood would give him the fancy camlet coat which the king vowed to wear while he lived. The young man shook hands in agreement that the king might have it, or any other thing he would ask for. "I was the more willing " admitted Norwood, "because he was the first king I could call to mind that had ever showed any inclinations to wear my old clothes." Norwood would wear his coat on his way to Virginia and then send it back to Kickotank when he had another, according to the plan. He had nothing with him to reward the two queens who had been so hospitable to him, but Norwood resolved to send them whatever gifts he could when he returned to civilization.

To the young princess who had been so kind, the Cavalier presented a piece of two penny scarlet ribbon and a small French manicure set he carried in his pocket. She was delighted with the gift and amazed that he would carry such a treasure hidden from sight. She went away for a while. When she returned she was wearing every individual piece of the collection. She added a bit of ribbon to the scissors, knives and other small tools, and they hung at her ears, neck and hair. The case was made into a decoration on her dress.

The Indian girl had also accented herself with dabs of paint on the end each of her fingers in alternating colors of green and yellow. As she stood before the

Parting Friends

guests she dramatically painted her face with the colors, beginning at her temples and continuing in an oval line as far as the paint would last.

"I could have wished that this young princess would have contented herself with what nature had done for her without this addition of paint" Norwood commented. The results of green and yellow stripes on the young face struck him as anything but pretty.

Norwood was told that only the royal family was permitted to use this form of ornamentation. He noticed that none of the other natives were painted in that way. This made him reconsider the painted princess in terms of her own culture. Since the decorations were a mark of royalty, the Cavalier learned to see them as lovely for that reason, as are "all things that are honored with the royal stamp."

Early the next morning a small group assembled to depart. The troublesome Major Stephens was in the party, along with three or four more. Major Morrison was greatly recovered from the ordeal, but not yet strong enough to make the long trek through the forests to Virginia. They left him and the remaining party, which included the two women who were also improving daily, thanks to the good care they received. Norwood told those who were remaining that the governor would send boats to bring them all to Jamestown as soon as it could be accomplished.

When breakfast was finished and Jack, the guide, was ready to set out, Norwood took a formal leave of the king. The two embraced in farewell, and the king expressed sorrow at his guest's departure. "I made Jack pump up his best compliments, which at present were all I was capable to return to the king's kindness," Norwood recalled, "and so, after many *Ha na haws*, we parted."

It was to be a much more tedious and difficult trip than Norwood envisioned. "We were not gone far til the fatigue and tediousness of the journey discovered itself in the many creeks we were forced to head, and swamps to pass which made the way at least double to what it would have amounted to in a straight line."

Norwood was amazed that the native guide could lead the way with absolute confidence about his direction, almost "as if he had had a London road to keep him from straying". Many times the Indian would stand still and look about for landmarks. An old deformed tree to the northwest opposite a small hill of pines to the southeast would be a signpost for him, no matter the weather.

The native had no knowledge of the compass, Norwood noted, yet always knew the northwest direction from the weather-beaten moss which grew on that side of every oak. It was different from moss on the rest of the tree. In the damp and storms of late winter, moss and lichen are even more apparent on the trees. The dreary light of a cloudy day can make the bright green almost glow against the neutral tones of the background.

Norwood and the others followed the Indian along a slight path through the forests of oak and maple, holly and pine. Cypress knees, the anchoring growths of the trees' root structure, marked the swamps that had to be bypassed.

Toward evening they saw smoke in the distance. In the sparsely populated wilderness, it was a sure sign of an Indian town. Jack knew it to be the village of Gingo Tea-gue, set by the creek of that name. The group had been advised by the king of Kickotank that his brother, who was a king of Gingo Tea-gue, would provide them with hospitality.

After walking for more than eight hours, Norwood was almost too exhausted to eat the food that was set before them. "I was extremely tired with this tedious journey and it was the more irksome to me because I performed it in boots, (my shoes being worn out) which at that time were uncommonly worn to walk in". The weary traveler was given the distinction of being housed apart from the others because of the friendship he had made at Kickotank. He was also offered the first taste of all the foods served, although he noted that the variety was not as great as he had been given before.

The distinction of rank had its disadvantages too. Although Norwood was given the best of the food and sleeping accommodations, he was also pestered by the king's children who wanted gifts and presents "beyond what I was either able or willing to afford them". He was too tired from the long and arduous journey to be able to deal with fending off the young beggars. At length, he had Jack explain to them that he needed to sleep, and they would all have to leave him alone until morning.

The exhausted Cavalier fell into a deep sleep and

passed the whole night without waking. At about daybreak he woke up suddenly and it took a few minutes to remember who or where he was. He was confused and confounded to see an Indian maid close to his side. It was the king's eldest daughter, who had cut off all the gold and silver buttons from the coat even as he slept in it. This sight brought him fully awake, but he remarked that it felt strange, as if he was in the kind of enchantment in which knights in stories sometimes found themselves.

Norwood immediately called for Jack to tell the princess he resented her actions in trying to take what he would not give. The coat was promised to the king of Kickotank complete with all its buttons. Jack angrily told the woman he was scandalized that one of the royal families should stoop to steal from a guest. When the king of Gingo Tea-gue was given notice of the affair, he rebuked his daughter, and caused the buttons to be returned to Norwood.

Norwood found some small presents to give the king and princess, and after breakfast the group proceeded on their journey to Accomack. It was still about twenty-five miles to the Jenkin Price house by his estimate. The weather was dry and not as cold. The travelers set out provisioned with pone to eat on the trail,

Forest Trail

and there was plenty of good water along the way, but Norwood was reaching the end of his strength. "The uneasiness of boots to travel in, made me by much the more weary of the former day's journey, and caused me to enter very unwillingly upon this second day's work."

The small group quietly followed Jenkin and the Indian, Jack, along the trail through miles of dense forests. From time to time, they passed through open boggy ground where short winter-brown grasses provided stepping stone clumps to cross the wet spaces. After crossing what would later be termed Delmarva Bays, the travelers again entered the oak and pine forest.

The woods were quiet at the group's passage. After many hours of slow walking over what seemed like an endless trail, Norwood was too exhausted to hear the sounds of wild turkeys or deer if they had been right beside him. The Cavalier's thin-soled boots, designed for riding, were nearly worn out and becoming very uncomfortable. Each step was painful and the damp intensified his misery.

Late in the day Jack offered to carry Norwood, who admitted he would not be much of a burden since he had lost a lot of weight from the strict diet he had been on for many weeks. He declined the Indian's offer, however, and resolved to continue on his own until they reached English territory. "The hopes of seeing English ground in America, and that in so short a time as they made us expect, did animate my spirits to the utmost point."

Jack feared his guest could not make it. The Indian recommended that they detour to his aunt's town. She was the Queen of Pomumkin, and her lodgings were not far out of the way, he told them.

Jenkin Price firmly opposed that motion. He repeatedly assured Norwood that the journey's end was

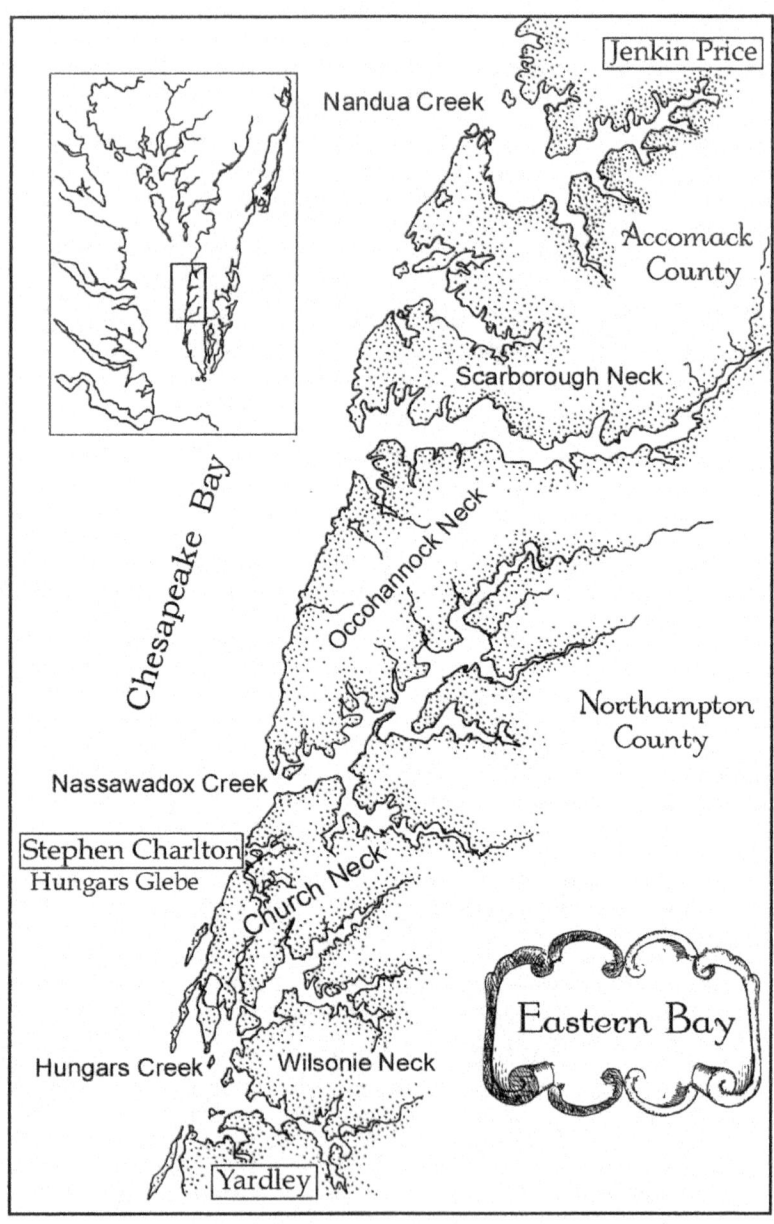

not far ahead. Norwood struggled onward in a haze of exhaustion and pain. "But the distance proved yet greater than had been described, and my boots trashing me almost beond all sufferance, I became desperate, and ready to sink and lie down."

Price lulled him on by telling him how close they were to his plantation. He pointed out the hogs and cattle that roamed open woods around them. Indians did not raise those animals, he said. It would be a shame to sleep outdoors on the ground within such a short distance from their goal. Norwood reluctantly agreed and stumbled on.

By the close of evening, a totally exhausted Norwood and the rest of the small group finally reached the Jenkin Price house. A large bed of sweet straw was ready for the traveler in the single room house. Almost immediately Norwood fell into it to rest his weary body. It was near the middle of February.   Since September the travelers had suffered storm, fatigue, peril and the extremes of danger on land and sea but they had at last reached the first civilized area of Virginia.

The homestead consisted of a small house built of roughhewn wood and a number of equally rustic buildings to serve as barns, sheds and animal shelters. Located on a tract of land owned by Samuel Littleton, it was near the Chesapeake Bay and convenient for transporting goods to markets farther south. Price traded with the natives in the area to supply beaver and other furs that were a major export to England.

Jenkin Price and the Indian, Jack, provided for their guests from the bounty of the farm. There was a dairy and hens to supply long forgotten milk and eggs. The visitors slept long and ate often and soon regained some of their strength.

Because of consistent growth to the north on

the Eastern Shore, the territory had been divided into Accomack county to the north and Northampton to the south in 1642, but at the time of Henry Norwood's visit in 1650, there were still few colonists north of Nassawadox Creek.

When he had recovered somewhat, Norwood began to look at the area around him. He was impressed. "It is," he reported, "the only country on that side of the bay belonging to the colony of Virginia, and is the best of the whole for all sorts of necessaries for human life."

The morning after their arrival was Sunday, and Norwood's small group would have liked to go to church to give thanks for their survival. There were no churches so far north on the Eastern Shore, their host told them, so once again the survivors held a prayer service among themselves as they had done throughout the journey.

The plantations of Virginia were scattered, and there were no towns of any size. Jenkin Price lived at the northern edge of the unsettled wilderness. Farther south, houses were closer together, but there were as yet few roads in any part of Virginia. Water provided the main transportation between farms and plantations set along the rivers and creeks that flowed into the Chesapeake Bay.

After a short stay with Price, the travelers continued their journey south by boat, to the more settled areas of Accomack where they met with universal hospitality.

Norwood was invited to many homes. The Cavalier was surprised that none would accept any compensation for food or lodging. "There are no inns in the colony," he noted, "nor do they take other payment for what they furnish to visitors." The Accomack community was glad to have such an important guest with news from England and the amazing story of his voyage

Hungars Glebe

with which to entertain them.

The travelers visited *Hungars Glebe*, the solid brick house of Stephen Charlton, built about 1643. The property was named *Hungars* from the Indian name for the nearby creek (and not a possessive term) and *Glebe*, from the English term for land grant.

The farm was a prosperous one and the visitors marveled at the variety of foods set before them. Charlton, who was an important community leader, also supplied Norwood with a badly needed change of clothes. That gave the Cavalier an opportunity to pack up the camlet coat, with the re-attached buttons, for delivery to the king of Kickotank. The Indian, Jack, made the trip back up the peninsula to deliver the the coat, along with other gifts for the natives who had been so kind to Norwood. After the trip Jack returned and stayed with the Cavalier. "He afterwards lived and died my servant." wrote Norwood.

After being well cared for at Mr. Charlton's home, the group of survivors was in a better condition to care

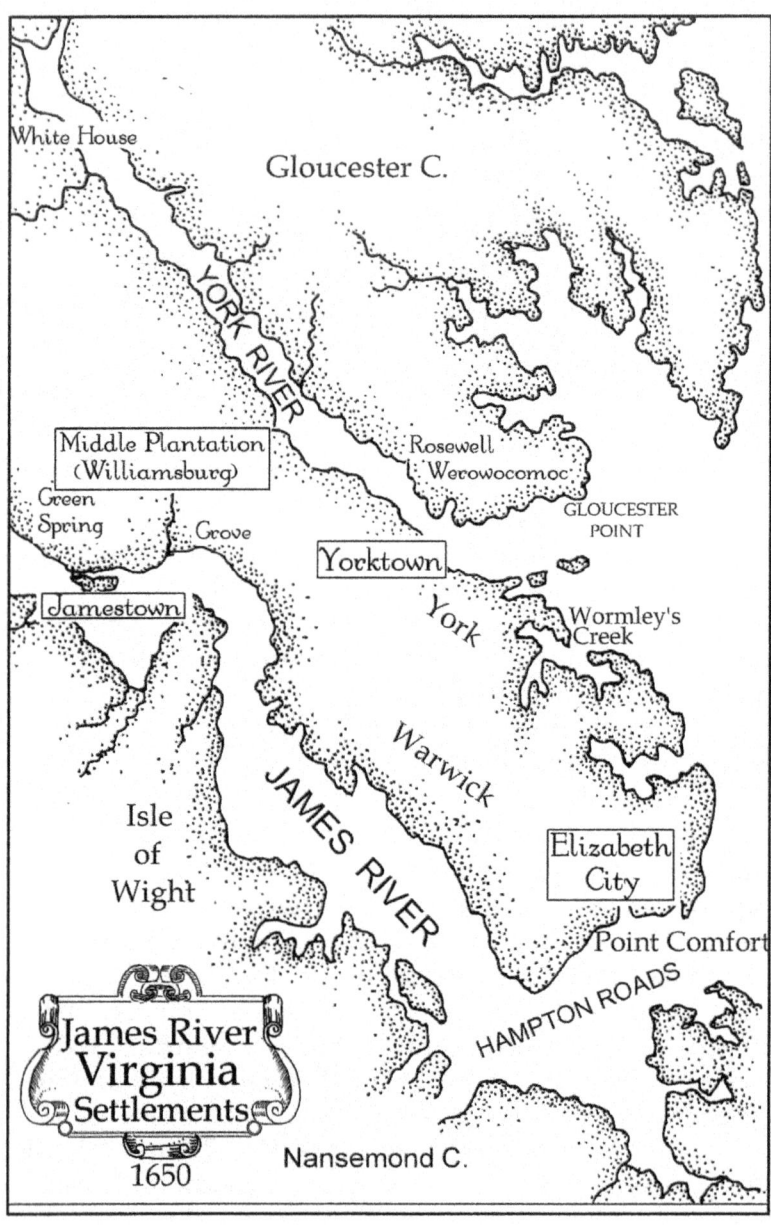

for themselves. They took their leave of one another, and each went his separate way. Norwood continued his journey to the home of Argoll Yardley, whose father had been governor of Virginia. There he was given an almost royal welcome.

Yardley recently had married and brought his wife from Rotterdam. Norwood had known the former Mary Custis almost since she was a child. When she came to Virginia after her marriage, her brother, John Custis, came with her. He was establishing himself as a colonist in Virginia.

The father of Mary and John Custis kept an important tavern in Rotterdam and was an influential man among the exiled English royalists there. Norwood knew the family well. Because of this connection with Virginia, Norwood was treated more like a relative than a guest. He stayed with the Yardleys about ten days in their spacious home on a neck of land facing Mattawoman Creek. He was feasted and entertained not only by them, but by all the neighbors in the vicinity.

Close to the end of February Henry Norwood departed the Eastern Shore at last. He sailed down the creek and crossed the Chesapeake Bay in the *Dolphin*, a sloop owned by a Dutch trader. On the western shore, at the dock of Ludlow's plantation on the York River, he was welcomed and offered accommodations. Norwood thanked Mr. Ludlow but declined the offer. He had heard that some old friends were nearby.

Less than an eighth of a mile from Mr. Ludlow's plantation, Captain Wormley had guests who recently arrived from England, and Norwood was well acquainted with most of them. "Using the common freedom of the country, I thrust myself amongst Captain

Green Spring

Wormley's guests in crossing the creek, and had a kind reception from them all."

Norwood met Sir Thomas Lundsford, Sir Phillip Honywood, and Colonel Hamond, who were among others at Captain Wormly's home. They were very pleased to see their thin and haggard friend. Henry Norwood recounted his adventures, and they celebrated his return to civilization into the night.

In the early morning Norwood was eager to be off to see the governor. Captain Wormly gave Norwood use of a horse and set him on the road southwest. The road passed through the growing village of Middle Plantation, later renamed Williamsburg. The governor's home at Green Spring was just a few miles from Jamestown. The road was not a long one but Norwood was glad to be riding a horse instead of walking on his still sore feet.

When he finally arrived at Green Spring, Henry Norwood was welcomed heartily by Governor Berkeley as a long lost relation, which he certainly was. The Cavalier's voyage to Virginia, expected to last only six or eight weeks had instead been nearly five months of discomfort, desperation and adventure.

Weeks later, when the weather made it possible, a ship was sent to pick up the travelers who had remained with the Indians. Presumably the ship went around to the Atlantic side of the peninsula and perhaps picked them up near the island where they had been lost.

Norwood spent several months with the governor's family at Green Spring. The manor house, built about 1648, was one of the largest in the colony. Located on a hill in sight of the James River, the house was a large two-story structure and featuring leaded glass windows, a luxury in that time.

With acres of land planted in tobacco and other crops, work had begun on walkways and terraced landscaping. A small structure at the back of the house protected the sweet water spring that gave the house its name and many outlying buildings served the functions of a busy plantation.

Inside the governor's mansion, the family's ornate furnishings from England made the surroundings seem only slightly more rustic than a manor house in Gloucestershire.

Berkeley was known for his hospitality and generosity to exiled Cavaliers, and Green Spring was a meeting place for all the important men who came to consult with the governor. Much of the business of the colony was conducted at the governor's home since there were as yet no official governmental offices. Norwood joined the gatherings to discuss the problems of the day.

Virginia was in a precarious position as far as the Civil War in England was concerned, and it was often a subject of discussion. While Parliament had successfully taken control of England, it had not yet turned its attention to Virginia. The colony, settled by Royalists, refused to accept Parliament's authority.

While most settlers were more interested in the practical concerns of farming and business, some of the younger Cavaliers still plotted ways to help King Charles regain his father's throne. While Norwood rested at Green Spring and recovered from his winter ordeal, he made friends and contacts among Virginia's Royalist exiles.

He had firsthand knowledge of the king's position and told them of the desperate need for funds with which to finance rebellion. When he had last seen Charles, a pact with Scotland seemed probable, and with it, a foothold on English territory. Norwood, with his colorful adventures, was a romantic hero to young Royalist Virginians, and they listened intently.

In late spring, Governor Berkeley recommended that Norwood return to Holland to find the king and solicit His Majesty for the position of treasurer for Virginia.

William Claybourne, who had long been treasurer, had proclaimed for Parliament, so was considered to have given up that post, explained the Governor. Norwood was working in support of the crown and a governmental position would ensure the king of further funds from the colony.

Norwood recorded that Berkeley was not only kind to him who had a blood kinship, but also to any Royalists who made Virginia their refuge. "His house and purse were open to all who were so qualified." he said. Berkeley was generous to Norwood's friend, Major Fox, who had no relations in the colony. To Major Morrison, the Governor gave command of the fort at Point Comfort. The fort was an important line of defense against enemy ships that might attempt to go up the James River to attack the colony.   The command was a profitable position while he held it for the king, and afterwards Major Morrison became involved in the government of Virginia

Seven

Farther Journeys

In May of 1650 Norwood once again boarded a ship and this time sailed west for England carrying letters and bills of exchange from Berkeley. Since it was usually inconvenient to carry gold or other cash, bills of exchange were used for most business. For transactions involving Virginia, a bill of exchange represented a quantity of tobacco and could be traded or sold for gold or other commodities.

After an uneventful voyage of about eight weeks, Norwood arrived in The Netherlands to find that the king was no longer there. Charles had gone to Scotland a few weeks earlier with hopes of being officially crowned as King of the Scots.

While he was in Amsterdam, Norwood met with Richard Glover, a British merchant, whose acquaintance he had made in Virginia. Glover gave Norwood money in accordance to the bills of exchange from Berkeley. The remaining credit was to be entrusted to Edmund Custis according to instructions from Norwood.

While Norwood was away on his trip to Virginia, Oliver Cromwell had solidified his control of England.

The Scots still stood against parliamentary rule, and there were pockets of resistance in the west of England. In 1648 Oliver Cromwell and Thomas Pride purged the Parliament of members who opposed their policies. The Rump Parliament, as it was known, governed England through an executive council and was strengthening its hold on the country through heavy taxation.

Puritan ideals were made into law, but somber clothing, enforced churchgoing and other repressive laws were not universally popular. Christmas celebrations were made illegal, theaters were closed and dancing and most forms of amusement were forbidden under parliamentary rule.

In September of 1650, Henry Norwood finally caught up with the king at Perth in Scotland. The king's fortunes, never very high, were at a low ebb. The Scots were demanding more concessions before they would crown him as King of Scotland and support him in a planned invasion of England. Charles' remaining forces had been recently defeated by Cromwell in the Battle of Dunbar. Prospects and finances for the Royalists were lower than ever.

The king must have found Norwood's visit a welcome diversion from his troubles. Charles was entertained by a retelling of the Cavalier's adventures in the wilds of Virginia and encouraged by the promise of help from the colonists. He could only reward Norwood with the requested patent for Treasurer of Virginia, and so signed the document on September 22, 1650. The patent awarded Norwood the position of Treasurer of Virginia with the right to keep whatever quit-rents he could collect.

The quit-rents were payments that in feudal times would release a freeholder from service to the crown. In Virginia the quit-rents were collected from each landowner after he had been on the land for seven years. The rate was set at one pence for each cultivated acre. Since the colonists' lands had been granted by the king, the money collected went to the monarch, or to whatever purpose or person he directed.

Charles was planning an invasion of England with Scottish troops the winter of 1650. They hoped to organize an uprising of Royalist supporters in England to coordinate with the planned invasion and to bring about the king's successful return.

Under the Commonwealth, guns had been confiscated from any who might oppose the Parliamentarians. The money sent by Berkeley and the Virginians would buy weapons to secretly re-arm the English Royalists. Norwood was deeply involved in the plans to transfer money and smuggle guns into the country for this purpose.

Apparently, Norwood stayed in Europe for the winter. Having received his patent in the late fall, he would not have been eager to board another ship heading for the North Atlantic with winter nearing. He may have been present at the ceremony crowning Charles II as King of Scotland on January 1, 1651, but by spring Norwood was back in The Netherlands.

Edmund Custis met Norwood in Amsterdam in April. Norwood paid Custis 1000 pounds from the money sent by Governor Berkeley. The funds were intended to buy arms in Holland where Custis intended to charter a ship belonging to his brother and smuggle the weapons into England.

"Norwood went for England, being anno 1651 and thence to Virginia." reported Custis later. So apparently Henry Norwood was again on a ship headed for Virginia by the summer of 1651 and likely arrived in the James

River by late fall.

Some reports indicate Norwood took a shipment of weapons back with him to arm the colony against Cromwell's troops. It was to be a short stay. Ousted Virginia Treasurer William Claybourne and a Puritan moderate Richard Bennett were already on their way with a fleet sent by Cromwell to replace Berkeley and the Royalists in Virginia. They were accompanied by a squadron of heavily armed ships led by Captain Dennis. The ships had been hastily assembled and were short of soldiers but carried an impressive number of guns.

They sailed to Virginia by way of the Caribbean Islands where they had subdued Barbados for Cromwell and collected several hundred free and indentured farm workers to serve as soldiers. The progress of the armed squadron was slow and Virginians had time to prepare for the likely invasion by their own countrymen.

On hearing that the fleet was approaching, Berkeley raised a force of one thousand men. Assisted by Dutch vessels from the area, he prepared to defend the colony against Parliament's navy.

The conflict was resolved without bloodshed, however. On his way to Virginia, Captain Dennis had encountered a merchant ship heading for the same port. He forced the vessel to stop and they confiscated a shipment of goods belonging to two of the Virginia Council members. On arriving in the Chesapeake, Dennis informed the owners they could submit to Parliamentary rule or lose their goods. The shift of votes in the Council resulted in the surrender of Virginia.

In the Articles of Surrender of Virginia in March of 1652 moderate Bennett saw to it that terms were reasonable, and little changed for the colony except the leadership. For the next eight years Governor Berkeley retired to his home at Green Spring. With the return of William Claybourne Norwood lost any chance of registering his patent for Treasurer of Virginia. The terms of surrender gave settlers one year to swear allegiance to the Commonwealth or depart the colony. Norwood left.

There are no records of Henry Norwood's activities for the next two and a half years, but he probably continued in his attempts to arm the resistance in England. He was in his native Gloucestershire in the winter of 1654 when he was captured by Parliamentary forces. A search of his lodgings in London revealed a cache of weapons. The *Christmas Plot*, as it became known, intending to arm Royalist supporters, was apparently unsuccessful because of a lack of money. Henry Norwood was arrested and charged with conspiracy against the government.

A trial was held in London, and Custis and others were obliged to testify against him. He was found guilty of crimes against the state and sent to the Tower of London. The infamous prison was to be Henry Norwood's home for four long years. Finally, in early 1658 he was released on the condition that he leave England. According to some sources, he was deported to the colony of New Jersey where he lived for a while.

After Oliver Cromwell's death in 1658, his son Richard was made Lord Protector but the fires of Commonwealth had burned out in England. Parliament soon invited the exiled Charles to return and be crowned king.

When London exuberantly celebrated the return to monarchy in 1660, Henry Norwood was there. He was honored with a ceremonial position as Squire of the Body in one of history's grandest coronations as King Charles II was restored to the throne of his father.

Shortly after the Restoration, Norwood's patent as Virginia's Treasurer finally took effect. His friends, Francis Morrison and Thomas Ludwell, acted on his behalf in Virginia to collect the quit-rents for him. The position of treasurer and the tax money collected were considered prizes the king could award where he wished. In this remnant of the feudal system, there was no intention that the money collected should benefit the taxed.

In 1650, at the time the king made the grant, he may have felt there would not be much money collected from the distant colony and that Norwood's efforts to purchase and transport arms for the royal cause were well worth the price. Ten years later, in the flood of pressing royal business after the Restoration, the king forgot the Virginia quit-rents.

Henry Norwood did not go back to Virginia, but returned to military service under Charles II. In July 1661 he was given life appointment of Captain of Sondown Castle in Kent, an honorary post. In the same year he was commissioned lieutenant colonel of Lord Rutherford's regiment and Deputy Governor of Dunkirk in France. Dunkirk was a strategically important port town across the English Channel and belonged to England at that time.

Two years later, King Charles, in need of money, decided to sell Dunkirk back to France. It was a very unpopular decision in England. Norwood had the ungrateful duty of lowering the English flag at the Dunkirk garrison when his troops departed. It was a task he was never allowed to forget. His friends teased him, and strangers taunted him for carrying out the unpopular orders of the King. Most of the Dunkirk garrison was transferred to the North African port of Tangier across from Gibraltar, where Norwood was made second in command of a force against the Moors. Henry Norwood's elder brother, Thomas, who was also in the military, served under him at Dunkirk and in Tangier.

On orders from the Admiralty, Norwood left Tangier in 1664 to cross the Atlantic yet again; this time to New Netherlands. He was among the party who took over the Dutch colony for the British. The colony was officially renamed New York in honor of the King's younger brother, James, Duke of York.

About this time the same Duke of York sent an expedition to select a site for a manor house in the Americas. The place that had been chosen for a grand vacation home was one that Norwood may have recommended to the prince himself. The site, now Fenwick Island, was near where the castaway travelers had suffered in January of 1650.

Norwood left New York and crossed the Atlantic yet again as he returned to Tangier. There he was made Lieutenant Governor and Commander in Chief in Africa. Tangier was an important garrison with its location at mouth of the Mediterranean Sea.

Coronation Parade

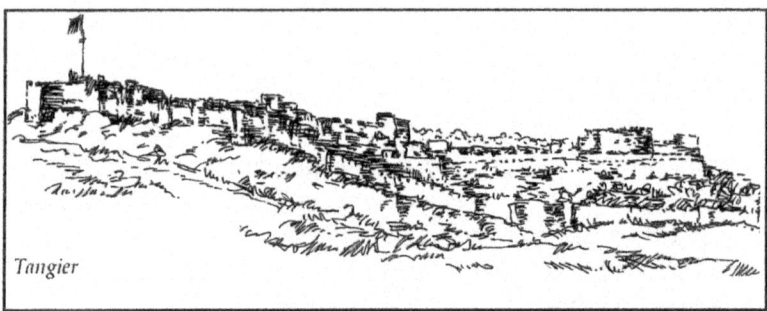
Tangier

In England, Norwood was not forgotten. Colonel Richard Nicholls had recommended Norwood for appointment as his successor as Governor of New York, but the position in Tangier was more profitable. Whether from his own choice, or a decision of the king, he remained in North Africa. In 1667 Norwood was even considered to replace his kinsman Berkeley as Governor of Virginia.

Norwood's post at Tangier was a stormy one. As lieutenant governor, he was often in opposition with the governor over policies. Samuel Pepys, who held an important position with the naval department in London, corresponded with him over several years and mentioned Henry Norwood a number of times in his personal diaries. Pepys wrote of the conflicts and complaints from the post at Tangier with which his office had to contend. After one meeting with Norwood in London where he had gone to report, Pepys wrote that he was inclined to take Norwood's side in a dispute with his superior.

According to one complaint, the Cavalier was accused of arranging for a woman from the sultan's harem to be spirited out of Tangier and returned to her home in Portugal. The action made Norwood some important enemies and nearly cost the English a valuable ally in the region.

At the close of his Tangier service in December of

1669, Norwood retired from active duty and returned to England with a certificate of commendation from King Charles. With the exception of four years in the Tower of London, and occasional visits on business, he had been away from England for nearly thirty years.

Henry Norwood returned to his native Gloucestershire a moderately wealthy man. With the proceeds of the Virginia quit-rents which had been collected annually and sent to him, he was able to purchase the ancestral home of Leckhampton Court from a cousin. He settled down to the comfortable life of a country gentleman at the age of fifty-four.

Three years later Lords Arlington and Culpepper secured a grant that gave them the quit-rents from Virginia. They recognized Norwood's interest, and privately arranged to give him a third of the profits. Eventually, Norwood sold his interest to Culpepper, as did Arlington.

In 1681, William Blaythwayt was appointed the Auditor General for America to find and collect money owed the government. He attempted to hold Norwood to account for the taxes he had collected for twelve years. Norwood fought the demand in court and successfully maintained that the quit-rents had been granted to him as a prize by the King. The charges against him were dropped.

Later that year King Charles was urged by the Privy Council to sign a declaration that he would no longer grant any individual the quit-rents so "that they might be reserved for the Support of the Government in the places aforesaid and they were originally intended." Never again would a monarch be able to award public tax money to an individual as a reward in the feudal manner.

For his dedication in serving the royal cause,

Norwood had profited well from his adventures in the wilds of America. For twelve years he collected a sizeable income from the royal quit-rents. The money enabled him to gain the home and social position that were important to him. He never married, but Leckhampton Court was his to fill with friends and relatives and collections from years of travel to exotic places.

After his return to England, Norwood was not ready to retire completely from public life. He served as Alderman and Mayor of Gloucester City for a while and as a Member of Parliament from 1675-1678.

He died in 1689 at the age of seventy-four and was buried in the Leckhampton parish church yard next to his grandfather. In his will he left the family home to his brother Thomas, who outlived him.

Henry Norwood also left a legacy for the natives who were so hospitable to the castaways. The story of his adventure, published as a broadsheet entitled <u>A Voyage to Virginia</u> is one of the few original accounts of those natives who once lived on the Eastern Shore of Maryland and Virginia. In writing his story, he saved for future generations a glimpse of the kind and gentle people who lived in harmony with the land at the end of an era.

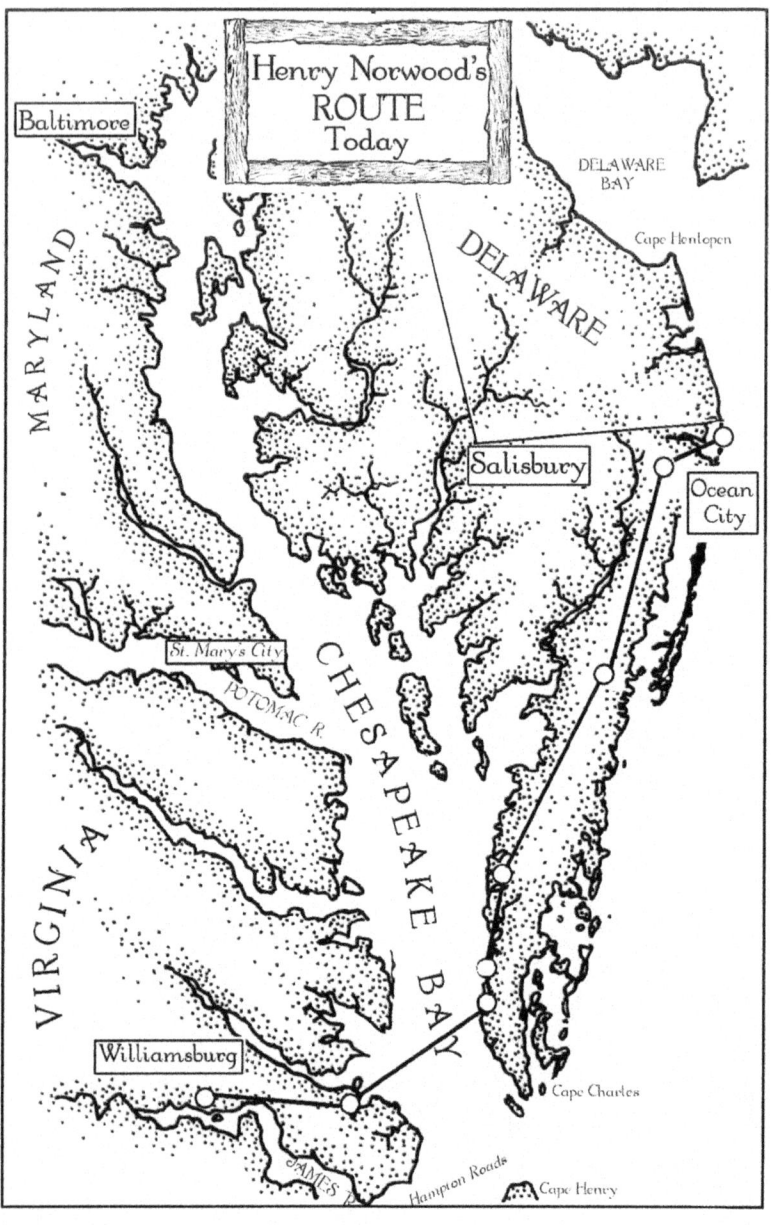

Epilogue

Today only names are left to remind us of the natives who once lived in the Chesapeake region. Settlers took many Indian names for rivers and towns, although colonists often did not know what they meant. Indian words became part of the colonists' vocabulary; *raccoon, moccasin* and *hickory* among them.

Lord Calvert's colony of Maryland claimed territory on the Eastern Shore of the Chesapeake Bay as well as the Western. The distinctions of Eastern and Western Shores were mentioned as early as 1631. The dispute between Virginia and Maryland over borders was partially settled later in the seventeenth century, resolving that the area Norwood visited in 1650 was on the Maryland side.

Like Virginia, Maryland also had laws against giving firearms to the Indians. According to the Maryland Assembly Act of 1650 "Noe Inhabitant of this Province shall deliver any Gunns or Ammunition to any Pagan for the killing of meate or to any other use upon payne of forfeiture to the Lord Proprietor 1000lb tobacco and loss of the partyes Gun to him that shall make seizure therof or

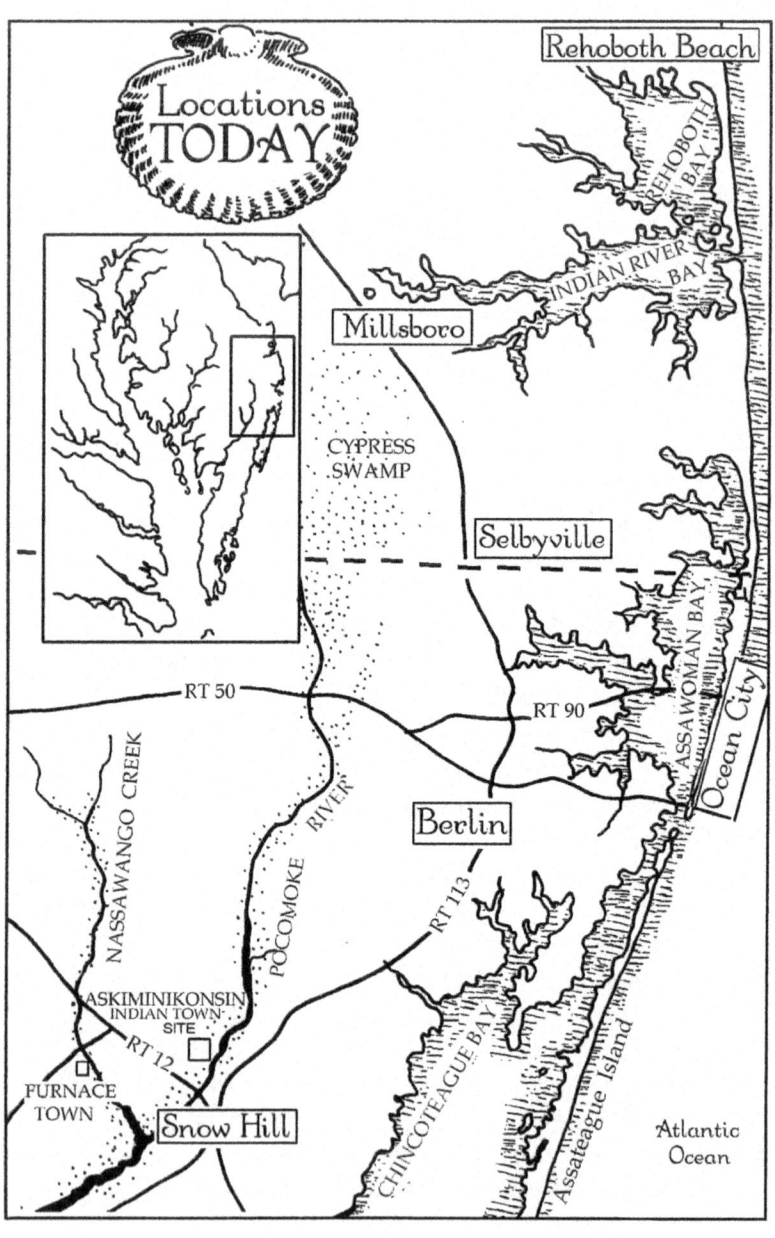

take the same from such Pagan or to him that shall informe therof and able to make proofe therof." The colonists often ignored the restrictions but it is probable that the firearms given as gifts to Norwood's hosts were not long in working condition in any case.

As colonists gradually moved into the area in the 1660s native tribes voluntarily or were forced to relocate their villages. The Kickotank group was displaced by the Buckingham land grant of 1679 which awarded 1500 acres of the area to John White. Although White did not settle on the property until a few years later, by the end of the century the tribe Norwood met had left.

They were probably members of the Assateague tribe although there were many small groups along the Atlantic seaboard whose existence and interrelationships were not known. The native king indicated that he was related to the king of the Gingo Tea-gue tribe and it is likely that the Kickotanks joined with them, along with scattered members of the Pocomoke, Assawoman and other tribes, in an Indian town called Askiminikonson on the banks of the Pocomoke River near the new town of Snow Hill.

The word *Askiminikonson* translates roughly as "stony place where we pick early berries" and possibly referred to the creek, now called Nassawango, that runs into the Pocomoke River. That creek, as well as some areas along the Pocomoke River, contains bog iron, certainly the only stones in a flat, sandy region. The early berries may have been shadbushes that bloom early in the spring. Shadbush fruits, also called serviceberries ripen in June and are the first of any edible fruit in the area.

Colonists often confused native place names. *Nassawango*, now the name for a creek, means "land between the waters" and probably originally referred to the roughly triangular area between the river and the creek. Indiantown was along the Pocomoke River within the Askiminikonsin reservation. Accustomed to moving over a broader area, the natives tried to maintain their tradition of hunting and gathering and simple agriculture.

In Accomack the natives were also moved from one area to another as the English enlarged their farms and new setters moved in. Many regarded Indians as third class people with less status than slaves. Rumors that the Indians planned to massacre the English colonists caused panic. Jenkin Price was with a group in April 1651 when Colonel Edmund Scarborough led about 50 men from Northampton County on an expedition to kill or capture the Queen of the Pocomokes. They shot at the Indians, burned their crops, and took prisoners, causing the natives to rise up angrily and turn against the colony.

Since it was against the laws of Virginia and the formal agreements made with the Indians, the leaders of the group were arrested and ordered to stand trial in Jamestown. Although they were forced to pay reparations for the damage they had done, the incident was largely overlooked, perhaps due to the social standing of Colonel Scarborough. The family name was an old and honored one, and his brother was a respected physician and friend of King Charles II.

Scarborough would have liked to kill more of the natives, but they seemed to melt into the forests and swamps when his band of raiders approached. He was quoted as saying that Indians were "easier to kill than to find." In 1659, through Scarborough's influence, Virginia applied to the Maryland government for permission to pursue the Indians in that province. Maryland declined, saying they did not know enough about the situation to permit it.

While violence was less a problem to the Maryland Indians, disease took a heavy toll on tribes in the region as natives had no resistance to smallpox and other European diseases. Their way of life was ten thousand years old, although archaeology indicates that these natives were in the area only since the 1400s. Colonists' land grants and settled farms curtailed the native practice of moving from place to place as they followed food sources.

Askiminikonsin was the largest Indian town in Maryland and was home to a number of tribes in 1686. By 1700 the population had declined however, and most of the remaining Indians moved north into Delaware and Pennsylvania, taking with them the bones of their ancestors. As the tribes dwindled, they joined with other groups and moved farther north, eventually into parts of Canada.

Some natives remained on the peninsula and eventually settled near Indian River, Delaware. It seems likely that the descendants of the Kickotank tribe are among them today.

While it is easy today to travel Norwood's route, exact locations for the sites he mentions are open to interpretation. The castaways probably landed near what is now 118th Street in North Ocean City, Maryland. There, where his group starved except for the oysters they found, modern visitors can order oysters in many resort restaurants. Those same oysters are more difficult to find along the shore. Where there were once banks and shoals of oyster shells, now bulkheads and docks mark the shoreline with unnatural angles.

During heavy midsummer rainstorms, water from parking lots and gutters spills across the highway near 94th street in Ocean City. This may have been the marshy

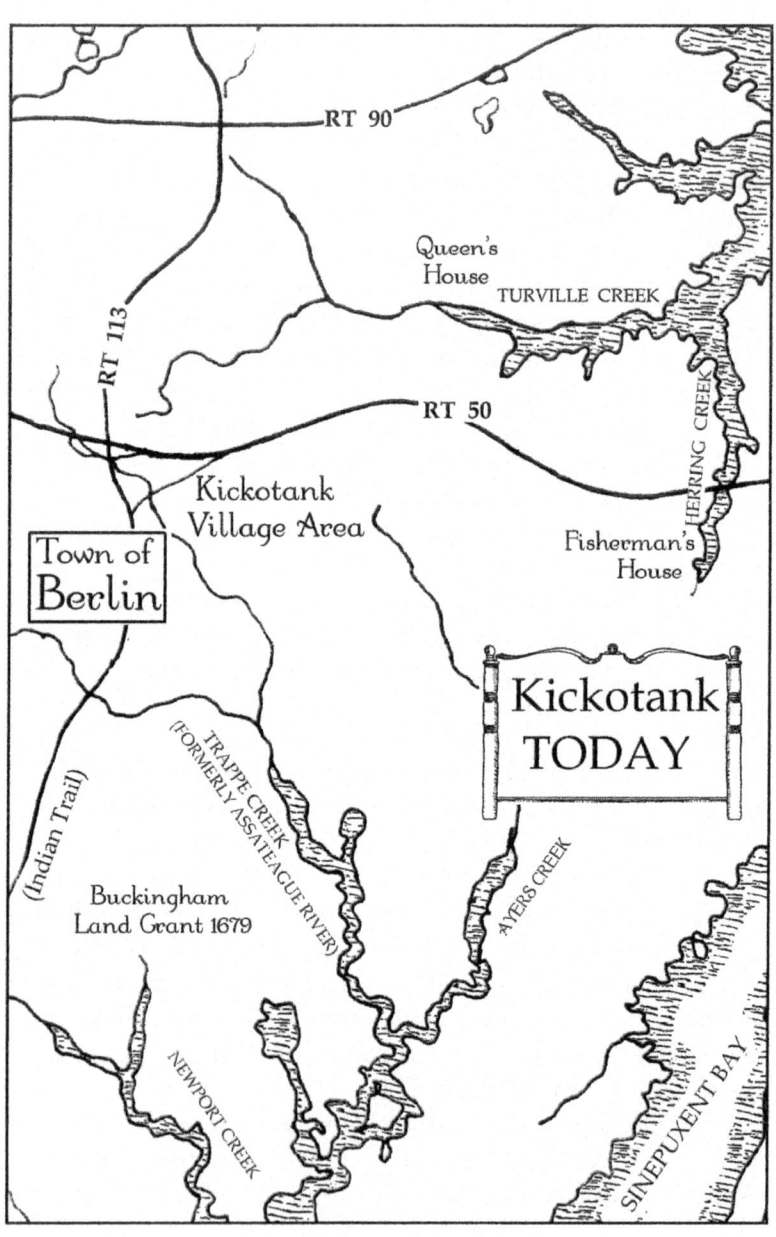

southern end of the island where Norwood helped the Indians launch a large native canoe.

Norwood recorded that his group traveled by canoe across the Assawoman Bay and entered a creek to the south. Today this is called Herring Creek in West Ocean City. Somewhere along the West side of this creek, farther south than where Route 50 crosses the creek, may have been where the starving voyagers first found refuge in the native fisherman's home.

Norwood's group went by canoe to their next stop. The dugouts probably returned to the mouth of Herring Creek and turned west into Turville Creek, another wide waterway. If they landed at the head of that creek as Norwood mentions, they would have been near what is now Ocean Downs Raceway. Higher ground on the north side of Turville Creek may have been a home site for the first native queen the group met.

From there, the travelers walked to the king's house. In his journal Norwood records that the king's home at Kickotank was five English miles from the fisherman's home and a half hour's walk from the queen. Using these estimates it can be assumed that the king lived near the present town of Berlin. Berlin was founded on what was the Buckingham land grant of 1679 and records indicate there was an Indian settlement there at that time.

The Buckingham patent describes a northern boundary of the Assateague River which is now called Trappe Creek. Native sites were always associated with a water source. The land has changed radically since Norwood's visit and the creek is probably smaller today than it was in the seventeenth century. The Kickotank Indian village may have been located in the vicinity of the Route 50-113 interchange just north of Trappe Creek.

When Norwood took leave of his native host and walked south accompanied by Jenkin Price and led by the Indian guide, Jack, he describes going through forests and bogs, but never mentions a river. It is more likely his group followed the Indian trail along the higher ground near the center of the peninsula thus avoiding the Pocomoke River to the west.

The Pocomoke River winds through dense cypress swamps whch are difficult to traverse, especially when swollen with winter rains. The Indian trail south from Kickotank had to cross through some parts of the swamp, but most of the route was over higher ground.

The woods are still home to a variety of wildlife. Wolves and bobcats are still occasionally seen but black bears are gone. Deer and wild turkeys have been reintroduced. Almost every forested acre has been cut many times in the last 350 years. Even in remote areas there are few trees near the size that Norwood must have seen.

Leaving Kickotank, the party walked eight or ten hours to reach the Indians at Gingo Tea-gue. The tribe whose name is now spelled *Chincoteague* did not live on the island of that name. Their winter home was along the Gingo Tea-gue Creek, now Mosquito Creek, near New Church, Virginia, and it was there that Norwood nearly lost his gold coat buttons.

The distance from the Gingo Tea-gue Indian village to the Jenkin Price home is 20 miles in a straight line. Following native trails through the forests would have been a lot farther. The Indian, Jack, suggested a detour to his aunt's house in the Indian settlement near the present town of Melfa. It was about twelve miles short of their destination, and the group was urged on. The modest Jenkins Price home was on the north side of the Nandua Creek in an area now known as Hacks Neck.

After resting at the Price home, the group proceeded to visit Stephen Charlton, an important man in Accomack. Charlton was a justice and spent two terms in the House of Burgesses. In 1650 he lived on 1000 acres south of Hungars Creek on the bayside west of today's Nassawadox. His home, Hungars Glebe, still stands.

It seems likely that Jenkin Price transported his guests to the Charlton home by boat rather than overland. There were few serviceable roads, and travel by water would have been easier on the exhausted travelers. At Charlton's home, Norwood sent the Indian, Jack, with his old coat and other gifts for his friends at Kickotank. In his account of his travels, Norwood mentions that Jack was afterwards his servant, so he must have made the return trip back to Accomack after delivering the gifts.

When the party went their separate ways at the Charlton house, Norwood went on to visit Argoll Yardley and his bride. No doubt he again traveled by water to the Yardley home which was northeast of the present town of Eastville.

If the modern traveler has no sloop to board, as Norwood did when he left the Eastern Shore, he must drive farther south and cross the Chesapeake Bay Bridge-Tunnel. This is the entrance to the Chesapeake Bay that the *Virginia Merchant* struggled to find and enter on her way to Jamestown. Cape Charles to the north and Cape Henry to the south, named for the sons of King James, have been outposts guarding this valuable waterway since the earliest days of Virginia.

When Norwood reached the Western shore he landed at Ludlow's plantation on the York River. By 1650 there were many prosperous plantations between the York and James Rivers. Norwood's friends were staying with Captain Wormley across the creek from the Ludlow plantation. There is still a Wormley Pond not far from the Colonial National Historic Park near Yorktown. From the Wormley home, Norwood rode a borrowed horse on the last leg of his journey to meet his kinsman, William Berkeley.

The site of Governor Berkeley's home at Green Spring is a few miles from the Jamestown Historical Park. Green Spring is protected by the state as an archaeological site, but little remains of the original house. The illustration of Green Spring house is based on the archaeological evidence and historical descriptions. Like Green Spring, Norwood's home at Leckhampton Court is no longer standing. The land, near Cheltenham, was sold in 1841 by another Henry Norwood, no doubt a descendant of the Cavalier's brother, and is now the site of a Georgian era bed and breakfast.

When the kindly Indian king of Kickotank called Henry Norwood "my brother," he meant it seriously. Natives often took on new names to commemorate special events in their lives and many Indians took English surnames in the late seventeenth century. Today *Norwood* is a common family name among native descendants living in the area of Indian River, Delaware. The friendship between two men from different worlds has survived the generations for three hundred and fifty years.

Bibliography

Ames, Susie M. 1973. *The Virginia Eastern Shore in the Seventeenth Century.* New York: Russell & Russell.

Amos, William H., and Stephen H. Amos 1985. Atlantic and Gulf Coasts. Audubon Society Nature Guides. New York: Alfred A. Knopf.

Arber, Edward, ed. 1910. *Travels and Works of Captain John Smith, President of Virginia and Admiral of New England, 1580-1631.* 2 vols. Edinburgh: John Grant.

Ashley, Maurice. 1971. *Charles II, The man and the statesman.* New York: Praeger Publishers.

Boorstin, Ruth F. (Editor) 1995. *The Daniel J. Boorstin Reader.* New York: The Modern Library.

Bridenbaugh, Carl. 1968. *Vexed and Troubled Englishmen 1590-1642.* New York: Oxford University Press.

Custer, Jay F. 1984 *Delaware Prehistoric Archaeology.* Newark, New Jersey: University of Delaware Press.

Dent, Richard J. 1995 *Chesapeake Prehistory: Old Traditions, New Directions.* New York: Plenum Press.

Feest, Christian F. 1990 Nanticoke and Neighboring Tribes: In *Handbook of North American Indians,* vol. 15 (Northeast). Ed. Bruce G. Trigger. Washington, D.C.: Smithsonian Institution Press.

Flannery, Regina. 1939. *An Analysis of Coastal Algonquian Culture.* Catholic University of America Anthropological Series 7. Washington, D.C.: Catholic University of America Press.

Hibbert, Christopher. 1968. *Charles I*. New York: Harper & Row.
Hutchinson, H. 1961. Indian Reservations of the Maryland Provincial Assembly on the Middle Delmarva. *Archaeolog* 13. 1-5.
Hyde, George E. 1962. *Indians of the Woodlands*. Oklahoma: University of Oklahoma Press.
Jackson, Melvin H. 1972. *Ships and the Sea: Voyaging to the Chesapeake*. New York: E.P. Dutton.
Meadows, Denis 1961. *Five Remarkable Englishmen*. New York: Devin-Adair Company.
Norwood, Henry. [1650]. *"A Voyage to Virginia."* In Tracts and Other Papers Relating Principally to the Origin, Settlement and Progress of the Colonies in North America, from the Discovery of the Country to the Year 1776, ed. Peter Force. 4 vols. Washington, D.C.: Peter Force, 1836-46. Reprinted, New York: Peter Smith, 1947; Gloucester, Mass.: Peter Smith, 1963.
Perry, James R. 1990. *Formation of a Society of Virginia's Eastern Shore* 1615-1655. Chapel Hill: University of North Carolina Press.
Quinn, David B. (Editor) 1982. *Early Maryland in a Wider World*. Detroit: Wayne State University Press.
Reay, Barry (Editor) *1974. Popular Culture in Seventeenth-Century England*. London: Croom Helm.
Roundtree, Helen C. and Davidson, Thomas E. 1997. *Eastern Shore Indians of Virginia and Maryland*. Virginia: University Press of Virginia.
Schmidt, Martin F. 1993. *Maryland's Geology*. Centreville, Maryland: Tidewater Publishers.
Whitelaw, Ralph T. 1968. *Virginia's Eastern Shore: A History of Northampton and Accomack Counties*. Gloucester, Mass.
Wedgewood, C.V. 1987. *History and Hope*. New York: E.P.Dutton.
Wright, Louis B. 1957. *The Culture of the American Colonies 1603 – 1763*. New York: Harper & Brothers.

Index

A Map of Virginia 92
A Voyage to Virginia 154
Accawmacke 116
Accomack 68, 160
Accomack County 136
Algonguian language 94, 105
Algonquin 102
Amsterdam 145
Andrews 44
Anglican 25
Antigua 31
Arlington, Lord 153
Articles of Surrender 148
Askiminikonsin 159, 161
Assateague 159
Assateague River 163
Assawoman (Indian tribe) 159
Assawoman Bay 86, 163
Atlantic Ocean 40
Azores 42, 43

Bacon, Francis xv
Barbados 31, 148
Barnstable 26
Battle of Dunbar 146
Battle of Naseby 26
Bennett, Richard 148
Berkeley Castle 21
Berkeley family 20

Berkeley, Governor William 29, 125, 140, 147, 148 166
Berkeley, Sir John 25, 27, 29
Berlin 163
Bermudas 53, 54
birding piece 119
Blaythwayt, William 153
breaches 54
Bristol 25
Buckingham 159, 163

Cabeco Gordo 43
cabuncks 90
camlet 93
Canary Islands 43
Cape Charles 69, 165
Cape Henry 69, 165
Captain of Sondown Castle 150
caragaroon 32
cartography xv
Cary, Francis 81
Cavaliers 22
Charles (king of Scots) 29
Charles I (king of England) 22, 25, 27, 28, 31
Charles II (king of England) 28, 30, 112, 142, 147
Charles, Prince of Wales 25, 27

Charlton, Stephen 137, 165
Cheltenham 21, 166
Chesapeake 148
Chesapeake Bay
 31, 68, 78, 80, 86
Chesapeake Bay Bridge-
 Tunnel 165
Chincoteague 164
Christmas Plot 149
Civil War 24
Claybourne, William
 142, 148, 149
Colonial National Historic
 Park 166
Commonwealth 29
cooper 40
Cotswold Hills 21
Cromwell, Oliver
 26, 28, 29, 112, 146
Cromwell, Richard 149
crotemen 110
Custis, Edmund 145, 147
Custis, John 139
Custis, Mary (Mrs. Yardley)
 139

Deal 35
Delaware 86
Delmarva Bays 133
Dennis, Captain 148
Divine Right 22
Dolphin (ship) *139*
Downs 35
Duke of York 151
Dunkirk 150
Dutch xvi, 81
Dutch States General 28

Eastville 165
Edward II (king of England)
 21
Elizabeth I (queen of England)
 20
English Channel 35, 40
English Civil Wars xiv
Escurial 101

Faial 42, 43, 45
Fenwick Island 86, 151
fore-topmast 59
fore-topsail 55
forecastle 40, 60
Fox, Major Richard
 30, 53, 142
France 27
Furnace Town Historic Site
 xvii

Galileo xv, 91
Generall Historie of Virginia
 92
Gingo Tea-gue 131, 159, 164
Gloucester 20
Gloucester City 154
Gloucestershire
 21, 30, 38, 141, 149, 153
Glover, Richard 145
Goldsmith's Hall 30

Gravesend 33
Great Migration 38
Great Shellfish Bay 78
Green Spring
  140, 141, 149, 166
Gregorian calendar xiv
Gulf Stream 53, 54

Hacks Neck 164
Ha-na Haw 95, 130
Hague 28
Hamond, Colonel 140
Harman, Thomas 81
Hatteras 54, 57
Henrietta Maria, (queen of England) 27
Herring Creek 163
Holland 28, 38
hominy 106, 108
Honywood, Sir Phillip 140
Horta 43, 45
House of Commons 25
Hungars Creek 165
Hungars Glebe 137, 165
Huygens, Christian 91

indentured servants 38
Indian River 161, 166
Ireland 29
Ironsides 26
Isle of Wight 27, 31

Jack (Indian)
  126, 127, 137, 164
James, duke of York 27, 151
James I, king of England 165
James River
  31, 32, 80, 141, 147
Jamestown
  20, 31, 80, 83, 112, 126
Jamestown Historical Park 166
Jersey Islands 27
John (king of England) 21
John (ship) 44
Julian calendar xiv

Kegotank 105
Kickotank 96, 105, 164
Kirton, James 20

Leckhampton Court
  20, 21, 153, 166
Leckhampton Hill 21
Leeward Islands 31
Lisbon 44
Littleton, Samuel 135
Littleton's Plantation 127
Locker, Captain John 32
London 24, 33
longboat 46
longitude xv, 41
Lord Baltimore 86
Lord Calvert 157
Lord Culpepper 153
lovelock 22

Ludlow 165
Ludlow's plantation 139
Ludwell, Thomas 150
Lundsford, Sir Thomas 140

Magna Carta 21
Malaga 69, 72
map makers xv
maps xvi
Mary (sister of Charles II) 28
Maryland 86
Massachusetts 29
Mattawoman Creek 139
Melfa 164
Menados 113
Middle Plantation 140
Milton, John xv
mizzen 58
Monte da Guia 43
Moors 151
Morrison, Major Francis 27, 30, 77, 78, 87, 113, 129, 142, 150
Mosquito Creek 164

Nandua Creek 164
Nassawadox 165
Nassawadox Creek 136
Nassawango 159
navigation 41
Netherlands 27, 145, 147
New Amsterdam 81
New Church 164
New Jersey 149
New Model Army 26

New Netherlands 151
New World xvi
New York 81, 113, 151
Nicholls, Colonel Richard 152
Norman 21
Northampton County 136, 160
Norwood, Elizabeth 20
Norwood, Henry 19, 25, 29
Norwood, Henry Esq. 20
Norwood, Thomas 21, 151
Norwood, William 20, 24
Ny a Mutt 109
Ny Tops T'op 93

Oath of Allegiance 30
Ocean City 87, 161
ocean currents xv
Ocean Downs 163
Oxford 20

Paris 27
Parliament 22
Parliamentary Committee 30
Pepys, Samuel xv, 152
Pico Island 44
Pocomoke 159
Pocomoke River 164
Point Comfort 142
pone 106, 108
porpoises 58
Portugal 44
Portuguese Governor 45
Price, Jenkin 125, 126, 132, 135, 160, 164

Pride, Thomas 146
Privy Council 153
Protestant Reformation xiv
Puritan 23
Putts, Mate (sailor)
  54, 55, 59, 60, 68, 69, 76, 77, 80
Pycaroes 49

Queen of Pocomokes 160
Queen of Pomumkin 133
quit-rents 146, 153

Reasin, Thomas
  55, 62, 65, 67
Restoration 150
rockahominie 108
Rodney, Sir John 20
Rotterdam 27, 139
Roundheads 22
Royal Exchange 32
Rubens xv
Rump Parliament 146
Rupert, Prince 51
Rutherford, Lord 150

satellite imagery xvi
Scilly Isles 27
Scotland 145
Scottish Presbyterian Church 25
scurvy 88
Severn Estuary 21
Shakespeare xv

Smith, Captain John
  19, 91, 96, 105
Smith, John (sailor) 55
Somerset 20, 21
Spain 27
Spanish moss 109
sphagnum moss 109
Squire of the Body 149
St. Germain-en-Laye 27
St. Mary's City 86
Stephens, Major
  97, 103, 120, 129
Summer Islands 50
Surinam 31

Tangier 150
Tatam, Captain John 44, 46
Tenerife 43
Thames River 33, 77
Thurtan, Sir Edward 81
tobacco 33
Tower of London 149
trade wind 53
Trappe Creek 163
Turville Creek 163

Versailles 101
Virginia
  xvi, 20, 29, 32, 81, 139
Virginia Company 20
Virginia Council 148
Virginia Merchant (ship) 32-73
  83, 122, 126
<u>Voyage to Virginia</u> *xiii*

Wales 24
weroance 96, 105
Western Islands 42
whip staff 41
William (prince of The
    Netherlands) 28
Williamsburg 140
Wormley, Captain 139, 165
Wormley Pond 166

Yardley, Argoll 139, 165
Yardley, Mary Custis 139
York River 139
Yorktown 166

Sharon Himes is a writer, artist and illustrator with a special interest in the history and nature of the Chesapeake region. She is a contributing editor for several online magazines and her woodland paintings in watercolor
are nationally recognized. Her historic maps and illustrations in pen and ink celebrate the natural and cultural heritage of the area.

A resident of Worcester County, Maryland, she derives her knowledge of the area from exploration and research fueled by an enthusiastic curiosity. Himes' introduction to Henry Norwood's broadsheet A Voyage to Virginia, first published in the seventeenth century, led Himes to research Norwood and his times and to create original maps tracing his travels across what was then a very different Eastern Shore of Maryland and Virginia.

She was so excited by the discovery of Norwood's story and incensed that his part in the history of the region had been all but forgotten, that she pursued years of careful research which culminated in a comprehensive account of Norwood's 1650 adventure.

www.ingramcontent.com/pod-product-compliance
Lightning Source LLC
Chambersburg PA
CBHW061315110426
42742CB00012BA/2195